TOM and JERRY

FIFTY YEARS OF CAT AND MOUSE

T. R. ADAMS

FOREWORD BY
WILLIAM HANNA

CRESCENT BOOKS

New York

For Mark and Linda,
May Long Life and Prosperity Be Yours

This 1991 edition published by Crescent Books,
distributed by Outlet Book Company, Inc.,
a Random House Company, 225 Park Avenue South,
New York, New York 10003

Text copyright © Terryl C. Boodman 1991
Illustrations copyright © Turner Entertainment Company, Inc. 1991

ISBN 0-517-05688-7

8 7 6 5 4 3 2 1

Printed and bound in Hong Kong

CONTENTS

ACKNOWLEDGEMENTS

The authors would like to thank the many people on both coasts whose help was instrumental in putting this book together; who were as enthused about the project as we are, and who, told of our cut-throat deadline, actually believed us and rushed information and materials to us in time.

In particular: Irv Spence and Lefty Callahan for making the MGM Cartoon Department come alive again. Mike Kadlec at Hanna-Barbera Productions for the terrific tour and all the stuff. At Turner Entertainment: Cathy Manolis for the endless use of her copy machine and the generous loan of her time and expertise; Dick May and his capable staff for blowing things up just as requested; and Jerry Solowitz and Marianne Golsan for the special video allotment; Carol Postal for giving us the green light, and Erica Rapp for her lightning responses to our numerous requests. Ned Comstock at the University of Southern California Cinema Library for sending everything so fast, despite the holidays. Mitch Rose for launching the project and for being there throughout. And of course, Bill Hanna and Joseph Barbera for sharing their lives, their world, and their wonderful cat and mouse with us.

FOREWORD BY WILLIAM HANNA

In the spring of the year 1939, more than 50 years ago, Fred Quimby, the then head of the MGM Shorts Department, asked Joe Barbera and me, Bill Hanna, to come up with some new ideas for a series of animated cartoons for theatrical release.

A few ideas were kicked around, but the one idea that kept coming back for another kick was a thought about a cat and mouse. It seemed like a solid idea to both of us. A natural conflict, a cat after a mouse, a big guy picks on a little guy, sympathy for the poor abused mouse. Laughter and applause when big guy, cat, gets just deserts. It made sense to both of us. And so started 20 consecutive years of producing this cat and mouse series called Tom & Jerry.

Twenty years of fun, yes, a lot of gratification, yes. It was a big success, seven Academy Awards, all for the same two characters, a cat and a mouse. Such a thing had never happened before and has never happened since. We were then and still are proud of that accomplishment.

Fifty years later those same cartoons are still seen daily by millions of people all over the world. How come? They were funny! It was that simple! How simple? Well, we spent about six weeks working on each six or seven minute cartoon perfecting every phase of production from the very first thought clear through to the final mix. So it wasn't really *that* simple after all. It was work, fun work that paid off.

Probably the easiest part of the entire project was providing the voices. Tom would yell each time he got clubbed one way or another and that's all. Neither of the characters have ever spoken one articulate word in any of the theatrical cartoons we produced. When Tom did yell, and he did yell, and loud, it was me yelling my head off to provide that sound.

William Hanna

"PUSS GETS THE GO-AHEAD"

For the cat and mouse are Tom and Jerry, and this, of course, is a Tom & Jerry cartoon.

The ever-dueling duo have chased each other from the Hollywood Bowl to Hungary to outer space and back, and fifty years after their movie debut, are still going strong. Vintage Tom & Jerry cartoons still play at the cinema, on television, and are packaged for sale or rental on videotape. And, new cartoons are still being made.

Born in Hollywood, Tom and Jerry have captured the delight, and the laughter, of audiences around the globe, garnered enough Academy Awards to make any movie star selfishly smug, and starred in motion pictures, television and comic books. But their beginning, like Horatio Alger's, was a very different story.

A cat, large, gray and devilish, a Machiavellian glint in his yellow-irised eyes, and a mouse, small, brown, cherubic yet cheeky, chase each other around a kitchen, demolishing the ice box, ironing board, plate rail, a whole sinkful of dishes, and littering the floor with egg shells, dripping yolks and oozing jam.

The kitchen battle wages on, its final outcome unknown to the participants. But to the people watching in the warm darkness of the theater, there is little doubt as to the identity of the victor – it will be the little mouse.

The Golden Age of Hollywood

The year was 1939. Europe was caught in the icy grip of World War II. America was just creeping out of the formidable clutches of the Great Depression. The world was numb.

But in Hollywood, life

9

PROPERTY OF
M-G-M CARTOON DEPT.
Aug 8, 1939
DO NOT REMOVE FROM PREMISES

PROD. # 42

The original model sheet for "Jasper" in Puss Gets the Boot. *The rounded ears, slanting eyes and rough fur mark him immediately as the prototype Tom. Model sheets such as this were used as guides by all animators working on the cartoon to maintain consistency of the characters.*

was bustling. Drama and comedy, music and magic, poured from the sound stages and back lots of the Metro-Goldwyn-Mayer motion picture studios. Movie stars and stuntmen strolled the narrow streets in gaily colored costumes. Lights, sound booms, dollies and cranes perched among sets for Old West forts and futuristic cities. In the previous year, MGM's cameras had rolled on one hit movie after another: *The Wizard of Oz, Ninotchka,* and *Gone With the Wind* to name a very few.

These were the halcyon days of Hollywood, and MGM, like all other movie studios, was a kingdom unto itself. And like all fairy-tale kingdoms, the studio had a chain of vassals – in this case theaters – sworn unto fealty with its products alone. Loew's Theaters, for example, could show only

MGM movies, while theaters in the Warner Brothers chain could exhibit only Warner Brothers pictures.

This was sometimes hard on the individual theater manager who could not capitalize on a hit movie if it was not of his studio's make. If a studio had a string of flops, the local theater suffered along with it.

Within this golden age of studio rule, however, the moviegoer reaped many benefits. To help attract, and maintain, audiences, motion picture chains gave viewers a whole string of features in addition to the two movies which one's ticket price purchased.

There were newsreels, travelogues, serials on Saturday afternoons, occasional varied, and usually humorous, short subjects, and of course, cartoons. And every studio had its own cartoon stars.

Disney had achieved critical and popular success with Mickey and Minnie Mouse, and the gang over at Warner Brothers – Bugs Bunny, Daffy Duck and Porky Pig – had full employment. But MGM limped along with a variety of unindelible characters, none of whom seemed to catch on.

The studio had tried The Katzenjammer Kids, a syndicated comic strip, circa 1910, about a family of German immigrants, as a series, but it didn't have the right stuff. The eve of World War II, with Europe already bombed and blitzed, was perhaps not the best time to introduce a Teutonic cast of characters. Produced in sepia tones instead of the new and exciting Technicolor, The Katzenjammer Kids faded away after only a few episodes without a whimper from studio or audiences.

MGM put its cartoon factory staff back on single effort shorts. And Bill Hanna, who had been a director on the failed Kids series, was teamed up with animator Joe Barbera.

Neither had started out in cartoons and both had come to MGM by a circuitous route.

From Car Washing to Cartoon Directing

Hanna, born in Melrose, New Mexico on July 14, 1910, moved with his family to California about seven years later. For a time they lived on 69th Street in Los Angeles, next to the Pacific Electric Railway, which with its local and fast tracks was surely an exciting spot for a young boy.

The Hannas then settled in Watts, a suburb of Los Angeles, where Bill took lessons on the saxophone, giving him the musical background which would prove so beneficial in later years.

Once in junior college, he studied a mixed course of journalism and engineering, which was abruptly halted with the stock market crash of 1929.

The title frame for the cartoon that launched careers – not only Tom and Jerry's but Hanna and Barbera's. Mammy Two-Shoes, the mouse (and cat) bedeviled housekeeper, debuted here as well. Just dissolving into the title is the previous frame, which read, in this first cartoon only, "A Rudolph Ising Production."

The shadow of the Depression hard on his heels, he landed a job working with the engineers building the landmark Pantages Theater in Hollywood.

When that stint ended, there was nothing else. Hunting like so many others for any kind of job, he finally found employment washing cars at a service station on Sunset Boulevard.

But Bill Hanna had been clever, and during his job searching had interviewed for a position with the newly formed Harman-Ising cartoon studio. Now, after only a week at the gas station, the studio called and offered him a job. He took it.

The tiny Harman-Ising enterprise (consisting of only 20 to 25 employees) was housed above Silver's Dress Shop and a garage, one corner of which was appropriated by the animation studio and fixed up with shelves and a sink. After each cartoon had been recorded on film, the celluloid sheets, or "cels," on which the drawings had been inked and painted were taken by Hanna down to the garage and washed for reuse.

After a couple of months, he was promoted upstairs to the ink and paint area, where he quickly became head of the department. He also burned the late hours oil going over story ideas with Rudy Ising, a night owl who came in to work at noon and stayed until almost midnight.

Now his musical background came into play. Hugh Harman needed music and lyrics written for some of his cartoons and, just as in the popular movie melodramas of the day where the understudy takes over, Hanna was the only one in the studio who could do it.

Putting the music on exposure sheets, timing the frames to the music, was very much like direct-

In Puss Gets the Boot, *Jasper smiles as the mouse dangles from his winking eyelid. But his glee will be short-lived. In moments, he'll break a planter and its stand and be told by Mammy that he's a "good for nothing cheap fur coat" and will be thrown "O-W-T out" if one more thing is damaged.*

ing cartoons, and within a year of being hired as a cel washer he was a full-fledged cartoon director.

Soon he was not only directing but writing stories as well. His work came to the attention of Fred Quimby, who was setting up a new animation unit at MGM, which until now had been contracting its cartoons out to Harman-Ising, and he was hired as a fledgling director.

Meanwhile, across the continent, Joe Barbera was also making his way toward MGM.

An Innate Animator

Born on Delancey Street on New York's Lower East Side, March 24, 1911, Barbera discovered early that he had a talent for drawing. In parochial school he was the boy with the chalk dusted over his dark pants, for he was frequently asked to copy pictures from Bible texts onto the blackboard.

His drawing ability followed him through Erasmus Hall high school in Brooklyn and then abruptly was forced to take a back seat. The Great Depression had hit and Joe, graduating from school, found himself employed as a minion of the Irving Trust Company. An artist rather than a banker, he detested the job but dared not quit.

"I had to resort to something," he recalls, "so I went back to drawing. I used to love the cartoons in the *New Yorker, Saturday Evening Post* and *Collier's*, and I would sit at night and dream up ideas and draw them."

Then he discovered that one could submit these cartoons to the magazines, dropping them off one week and picking them up the next. Every day at lunch time, the minute the clock hit noon, Joe was on his way cross town.

"I'd zoom out at twelve, down the stairs, onto an express train, zoom up to 14th Street, 34th Street, get off at Grand Central, up the stairs, across Grand Central, up the stairs into Park Avenue, to Collier's Magazine, leave a new idea, pick up the old ideas, zoom over to Redbook, back on the train. Rejects every week. Then I'd go back to Wall Street and just get in, in one hour's time. Forget lunch. That's why I always weighed 128 pounds, I think."

Then one day he got a letter in the mail, a check for one of his sketches. At the tender age of 18, he was in heaven. Soon he was selling more cartoons, but still working for the bank.

In the meantime, he had become entranced with the art of animation, courtesy of a Disney film, and was taking night classes at the Pratt Institute in Brooklyn and the Art Students League in New York, at the high price of fifty cents a night.

An instructor at Pratt knew he was interested in animation and set him up with an interview at Famous Studios (the Popeye people), where he was offered a probationary position. Taking a vacation from the bank, Barbera was put to work as a painter, coloring in cels.

But after four days at the studio, learning that a fellow inker had been doing the same thing for two years, Joe decided to return to the bank. "That was the end of my career in animation."

Fate has a strange way of twisting one's arm, however, and shortly thereafter the bank, facing ever worsening economic conditions, laid off its bachelor employees in favor of retaining the young marrieds with families to support. Barbera was one of the newly unemployed, but not for long.

Walking out on Broadway, feeling like "the albatross had been lifted off my neck," he ran into a fraternity brother who sent him across the street to the Van Beuren cartoon studio.

Hired by Van Beuren as an in-betweener (the person who does the drawings in between the animator's key sketches), he went home every night and practiced drawing until almost dawn. When a group of friends went away for the weekend, Joe went with them, but while they were out skiing or sledding, he was up in his room, practicing on a portable animation board. Within six months the studio made him an animator.

When the Van Beuren studio lost its distribution contract with RKO Pictures and closed, he went to work for Terrytoons in New Rochelle, New York, and from there was hired by the newly forming MGM Cartoon Department in sunny California. And here, in 1937, Bill Hanna and Joe Barbera first met.

They had been at MGM for a year, however, before being paired on their first joint project, a seven-minute cartoon. It was a stimulating but short-lived partnership.

The cartoon, like so many of MGM's at the time, fell victim to the vagaries of the studio and the public, its animated stars now lost and long forgotten. Hanna went on to direct the sadly destined Katzenjammer Kids and Barbera went back to the drawing board as a staff animator.

Cat and Mouse Casting Call

Then, sometime in 1939, they teamed up once again. Their goal was to create a cartoon series, one in which the characters would live and breathe and leap off the screen, into the imagination, where they could go on, from one episode to the next and then on to the next, for years to come.

Hanna had been impressed from the beginning by Barbera's agility with a pencil. Under his hand, creatures and characters appeared quickly, magically, as if they were already on the paper and were waiting only for the pencil's touch to bring them to buoyant life.

As Jack Zander, a fellow animator, once explained, "He could draw a storyboard so fast that it would take two people to pin the drawings up on the board while he was making them."

Barbera, in turn, recognized Hanna's outstanding ability to direct.

Together, they fused into a dynamic team, one which took its self-imposed task of creation seriously. The first step was to develop characters with staying power; characters who would have

Production supervisor C. G. "Max" Maxwell and assistants check the animation for Puss Gets the Boot.

some intrinsic characteristic that would keep them
alive and lively, and would keep audiences coming
back for more; characters who would gain and
maintain definitive personalities.

After much thought, discussion and specu-
lation, they hit on the magic formula: two characters with an inborn, innate sense of conflict. These
could be a dog and cat, or a fox and dog, but somehow a cat and mouse seemed ideal. "I knew that no
matter where you ran it," Barbera recalls, "the
minute you saw a cat and mouse you knew it was a
chase."

Added to this innate sense of conflict was an
adage that dated back to the beginning of time – a
sense of justice. The little mouse never starts the
conflict; the big nasty cat does. And duly pays.
Although they trade insults and injuries throughout
the cartoon, it's the cat who gets it in the end, not
the mouse. Justice prevails.

Stars of the first cartoon having been cast,
Hanna and Barbera now sat down to draw some
rough sketches and write the story.

This done, they set their series prototype
before Fred Quimby, the head of MGM's Cartoon
Department, for approval. Quimby, however, did
not approve, being of the opinion that cat and

mouse cartoons had been done too many times
already. Hanna and Barbera could not possibly
come up with anything different.

Somehow they convinced him to give their
creations a chance, and the project went full speed
ahead.

That cartoon, christened *Puss Gets the Boot*,
tells the story of a cat who's on thin ice with sharp
skates. While chasing an innocent little mouse all
over the house, he breaks a planter and its stand, an
occurrence that is apparently not unusual. He is
warned by the housekeeper that he's on probation –
one more broken object and he gets the boot. He'll
be an outdoor cat, with none of the cushy privileges
inherent in the position of housecat.

Now the mouse is perfectly primed to upset
the cat's precarious position in the household. He
throws glasses off the sideboard, dishes off the plate
rail – anything breakable gets tossed to the floor.
The cat tries to stop the mouse not only from breaking things but from breathing. Havoc ensues, until
finally puss gets the boot.

This first cartoon got its debut on February 10,
1940 when *Puss Gets the Boot* opened in Los Angeles
to rave reviews. The adventures of Jasper (as the cat
was then called) and his long-tailed adversary were
also an instant success with movie audiences.

According to the *Motion Picture Herald*, the film
was "an especially clever portrayal of the smug
superiority of the cat dictator." The *Herald*'s re-
viewer, apparently swayed by Jasper's "superiority" seems to have overlooked the fact that the
mouse wins in the end.

As Tom and Jerry's battles continued, cat
lovers often accused Hanna and Barbera of feline
abuse. But, says Bill Hanna, "we have discovered
that the harder they hit, the louder they laugh. So
we didn't change our formula."

That formula was equal parts situation (i.e.,
conflict) and personality. And, Tom and Jerry have
very definite personalities. Tom is a fiendish oppor-
tunist, always anxious to ingratiate himself with the
powers that be, whether housekeeper, dog, or
even, on occasion, mouse; while Jerry, the impish
schemer, is happy minding his own business until

cornered, piqued or generally provoked.

The gags they pull on each other come directly from their personalities and therefore seem spontaneous, giving the cartoons a style that remains fresh story after story.

In fact, Tom and Jerry sometimes dictate the course of the action in a storyline. Although Hanna and Barbera were technically in charge of writing the scenarios, the sheer force of feline or rodent cause-and-effect could take over the pencil, sending the story off on another tack.

This may be why Hanna and Barbera consider Tom and Jerry to be more than celluloid characters; they think of their creations as real beings.

Ink and paint don't talk. Neither do Tom and Jerry. But they are nonetheless magnificent mimes, capable of nuances of expression and feeling that words cannot equal.

Their creators, along with their audiences, certainly fell under their spell, spending every evening

of *Puss Gets the Boot*'s six week Los Angeles run at the theater cheering them on.

Everybody else in the audience was just as delighted, but MGM, perhaps viewing Tom & Jerry's success as a flash in the pan, put Hanna and Barbera on a couple of musical cartoons, one with frogs and one with fish. After these intriguing but unrewarding riparian expeditions, Hanna and Barbera decided to go ahead with the next Tom & Jerry episode.

They sponsored a contest among the studio staff to rename the cat and christen the mouse, who, up to this point, had no name at all. Hundreds of names, in all conceivable combinations, were submitted. The winning combination, "Tom & Jerry," was passed over at least 50 times before it was finally

A later model sheet. Notice how their appearance has changed over the years.

chosen. "I don't honestly know how we settled on Tom & Jerry," Bill Hanna says now, but the fact is that they did. Perhaps the little team named themselves. No prize was given to the winner, fellow animator Jack Carr, except the pride of contributing to cartoon history.

Now that Tom and Jerry were officially christened, Hanna and Barbera went to the big cats at MGM with the happy news that a new cartoon was in the works – and were promptly rejected.

The minds of the MGM men were still stuck in the same gear. Too many cat and mouse cartoons – including, it seemed, Felix the Cat and Mickey Mouse (neither of whom had constant feline/rodent adversaries), and a crazy Terrytoon mouse – were out already, and nothing new or entertaining could possibly be done.

And nothing could be done to change their minds. Tom and Jerry were on the express bus to cartoon limbo along with the fish and frogs.

Then, a letter arrived from Texas. Besa Short, a heavyweight in the Loew's theater chain in Dallas, wrote to MGM to express her admiration for *Puss Gets the Boot* and to ask when new cartoons would be made. That turned everything around. Tom and Jerry were no longer destined to be cartoon has-beens.

And, by this time, the Academy Award nominees had been named. *Puss Gets the Boot* was in the

running. Between the clout of Besa and the promise of an Oscar for Best Short Subject, Cartoon, MGM was cajoled into giving the okay for not one but two new Tom & Jerry flicks.

In 1941, *The Midnight Snack*, a paen to refrigerator demolition, and *The Night Before Christmas*, a yuletide tale, were released. The latter garnered another Oscar nomination.

Tom & Jerry Come Out on Top

In 1943, at the apex of World War II, *The Yankee Doodle Mouse*, which showed off Jerry's imaginative military skill and ended in a burst of patriotic fervor, lifted Tom and Jerry from hopeful Oscar nominees to proud Academy Award winners, and put them firmly in the limelight as they continued to pull in Oscars for the next ten years.

The Yankee Doodle Mouse cemented Hanna and Barbera's position at the summit of MGM's Cartoon Department. The studio's usual operating mode was to have all cartoon makers report directly to Fred Quimby before going ahead with any projects.

At first, Hanna and Barbera, too, were required to get storyline approval from him, but a year before *The Yankee Doodle Mouse* made its debut, Quimby told them, "You fellas don't have to go over material with me. I know what you're going to make before you make it."

From that point on, says Bill Hanna, ". . . for 20 years Joe and I operated our own little niche in the studio, independent of any interference or direction from anybody at MGM. It was like we were our own bosses."

"Despite the fact," adds Joe Barbera, "that people said how many (Tom & Jerry cartoons) can you make, we made them for 20 years and that's *all* we did. And every one of them was a delight."

Jasper chases the mouse through the living-room, in a scene from Puss Gets the Boot. *Even at this early stage of their relationship, the little fellow has a cocky defiance in his run.*

Over the course of those many years, Tom and Jerry changed surprisingly little.

Designs on Tom & Jerry

Every two years Hanna and Barbera pinned sketches of the current Tom & Jerry "models" to the wall of their office, examining them, like Detroit auto manufacturers, for necessary or desired design modifications, but their changes were subtle.

In the first cartoons, Tom and Jerry had an indefinably rubbery, elastic, slightly amorphous appearance that is quite different than the more sharply defined, almost streamlined features granted them in later years.

Infinitely charming, the original Tom and Jerry moved with a kind of sprightly fluidity that dates them back to the pioneer days of cartooning. Over the years their kinetic style, always realistic, ever effervescent, grew less elastic and even more lifelike.

Over time, Jerry put on some weight, gaining a chubbier tummy and a cuddlier look, and he lost the long eyelashes that matched his whiskers, but otherwise he remained the same loveable scamp he had been from the first.

Tom's fur was originally rough around the edges, with a jagged, sawtooth appearance. This was the accepted way to indicate cat fur at that time. But it led to a certain dizziness for viewers as the jagged points of fur, different in each frame of film, jounced around on the animal's back. As Joe Barbera points out, "when you do 12,000 drawings and the cat has got (sawtooth fur) on him all the time, they dance, you see, they jiggle."

After the first few cartoons, Tom's fur smoothed out, while conversely, his already wild eyebrows grew wilder as he grew into them.

In addition, his gray ears eventually became pink inside, and his white face grew into gray with just a white muzzle for contrast.

Although Tom and Jerry's appearance, like all of ours, changed over the years, one thing did not: their ability to entertain.

Joe Barbera and Jerry Mouse, Tom Cat and Bill Hanna. "We always looked at both of them as human beings," says Hanna. "So did we," agrees Tom.

Just how they achieved that goal is a secret, perhaps not entirely known even to their creators, for one of the tenets of star power is its inherent, magical, magnetism.

What is known, however, is how they came to life through the talents of Hanna, Barbera and their staff of animators, who, like ancient alchemists changing lead into gold, wrought life from ink, paint and paper.

Much Ado About Animating

More stars than there are in heaven, MGM proudly proclaimed of its stable of actors, and no one could deny that Tom and Jerry were among that heavenly firmament.

They danced divinely, sang on occasion, spat, made up, kissed, fought, and generally bashed, crashed, smashed and walloped each other across the movie screens of the world. But how did they achieve all this when they were, essentially, two dimensional drawings on sheets of celluloid?

To discover their secret, one must turn back to the place of their creation, the MGM main lot in Culver City, California. Here, in a round-cornered, two-story, cream-colored stucco building containing a rabbit warren of rooms for animators, layout artists, in-betweeners, ink and paint girls, cameramen and movieola machines, Tom & Jerry leaped magically to life.

Here, too, were created the beaches, backyards, kitchens and castles in which they wreaked their havoc and the situations which put them there.

Each cartoon started with an idea dreamed up by Hanna and Barbera at brainstorming sessions in their office. Seated across from each other at a big table, they bounced story ideas back and forth like participants in a mad tennis match, until one hit with sufficient force to strike a funny bone.

Sometimes the idea was only a title. For example, as Joe Barbera explains, "The idea is a cartoon called *The Bowling Alley-Cat*. Well, why not? It's a funny title."

Out would come the ever-present pencil and paper, and Joe would start making little thumbnail sketches, each scene blossoming magically on paper as quickly as it was discussed.

Thumbnail sketches for The Bowling Alley-Cat *done during a recent interview with Joe Barbera.*

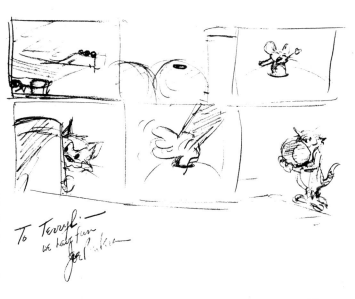

"For instance," continues Joe, "you have a drawing, so you figure, what do you do in a bowling alley? Here's the rack, where the balls come back. There's a few balls up here on the rack, here's your alley, maybe some more balls here. And it's night-time. That would be my first drawing.

"Then the next drawing . . . the camera moves in and we cut in close. Now, why am I doing that? Because I know there's a hole there.

"Then my camera moves even in closer . . . This is a real close-up of the bowling ball. And who comes up, naturally, yawning, arms stretching, but the little mouse.

"Then we cut to the corner, and around the corner comes, who else? Mr I'll Get You/I've Got You Now, Pal. This is the cat.

"Now the mouse makes a take and ducks in. And the cat puts his thumb in the hole. Then of course he's going to pick the thing up and he's got the mouse in there and he's squinting down the alley and he's gonna throw that poor guy in the ball. And he's smiling, naturally.

"But remember the cardinal rule was that the little mouse is not bothering anybody. The cat's the guy and so whatever happens to him . . . Plenty happens to him."

And Joe's lightning pencil sketched out exactly what did happen to Tom Cat. As the scenes were penciled in, detailing each sequence of the cartoon from fade in to fade out, a storyboard was born.

The Storyboard

The storyboard is a film script in picture form, each illustration showing peak points of interest, close-ups, pans, and beginnings and payoffs of gags, and is a very necessary device in the world of animation.

Where the director of three dimensional actors has the luxury of being able to shoot his stars from different angles with different cameras, later combining and editing each camera's film to final perfection, the animator must do all his editing before any drawings are done. His characters' thoughts, gestures, actions and antics must be carefully planned ahead of time; the amount of time necessary to draw, animate, ink, paint, and photograph

A storyboard for Jerry's Cousin. *The drawings, while quick and unpolished, still get each point across vividly.*

A timing, or exposure, sheet. The action is described verbally in the lefthand column and by frame in the middle columns. Notice the sketches in the righthand column.

A frame from the finished cartoon. The signpost, propelled by a speeding Tom and Jerry, is spinning exactly as described on the timing sheet. It has suddenly sprung to life.

each seconds-long sequence brooks no room for changes in midstream.

While cartoonists have used the storyboard since its invention by the Disney people in the 1920s, Hanna and Barbera were unique in their ability to "write" the storyboard at the same time they were "writing" the gags; in effect, using a sort of sketch shorthand to eliminate the step of typewriting a script, then going back days later and putting it in storyboard form. This magical ability kept the gags, and the story, as fresh and spontaneous at the end of the planning stage as they were at the exciting moment of inception.

And the gags dreamed up for Tom and Jerry were very creative. "Gags" meant anything from a simple bash on the head with a hammer to a Rube Goldberg sequence of events, such as the following from *Nit-Witty Kitty*:

Tom, believing due to a bump on the head that he is a mouse, chummily urges a piece of cheese upon Jerry. Jerry, exasperated by Tom's delusion, throws the cheese in the air. It flies up, eventually landing in an egg cup on a plate rail. The cup twirls, falls over, rolls along the plate rail, hits a plate, and knocks it off the rail. The plate tumbles down and lands in a clothes basket resting on a chair. The basket topples to the floor, the plate rolls out, spins across the kitchen floor and hits a broom. The broom falls forward, its handle hitting a latch on a cupboard door. The door opens and an ironing board falls out, smacking Tom square on the head.

The action goes from Tom to Jerry through this entire complex sequence and ends where it started, with Tom.

The chain of events is delightfully well thought out – what sort of objects are found in a kitchen, how they work, and how they can be used to best effect by cat and mouse.

While the gags flew across the table between Hanna and Barbera and were skewered to the drawing page by Joe, Bill too was scratching away with pencil on paper, timing the unfolding cartoon, or, in other words, practicing the arcane art of directing animated actors.

Two Dimensional Directing

Live actors can be verbally instructed to speak slower or faster, to run instead of walk, to give a humorous situation more punch by staring long and hard at a wall after walking into it. The cartoon star, while able to emote every bit as eloquently as his three-dimensional counterparts, is given his direction through the use of a timing, or exposure, sheet.

This is an 8½ by 14 inch piece of paper ruled neatly across like a school tablet and divided lengthwise into four long columns. On this graph, the director indicates how many frames, or drawings, will be required for each action. One second of on-screen film uses 24 frames, or 24 separate pictures. The fewer the drawings, the faster the action. Jerry scurrying across the room, Tom hot on his heels, might require three frames for him to take one step, whereas Jerry tiptoeing slowly across the room while Tom sleeps might take up to 12 frames per step.

Each line on the graph represents one frame, while each vertical column represents a different action or character. Spike sleeping on the living-room rug, Jerry scampering and Tom stalking all will require a different pace and therefore a different celluloid drawing, which will be layered one on the other when the cartoon is filmed.

Timing is also critical to the cartoon's raison d'etre, the laugh. The speed of a run, the slowness of a double take, all contribute to the characters' ability to amuse.

In *Tee for Two*, while playing golf, Tom tees off and, to his smug delight, hits the ball, which immediately ricochets and returns to hit him in the mouth.

"He's got the big grin," says Bill Hanna, "all teeth, and the ball goes through and breaks a hole. Now when it breaks the hole, it makes a crack and then pieces continue to fall out of his mouth. That timing is critical to a laugh."

The timing of this sequence, from the rapidity of the ball sailing back toward Tom to the freeze frame, or hold, while Tom registers surprise that his golf ball would dare do such a dastardly thing, to the quick succession in which his teeth tumble out of his frozen grin, all were laid out by Bill on the exposure sheet.

Meanwhile, he explains, "Joe would be the one drawing the cat with the big grin and the hole in the mouth and the pose for the golf swing."

Now Hanna and Barbera went on to the next sequence of the story, frequently laughing aloud as they worked. Creating new trials and triumphs for Tom and Jerry was an ongoing delight from which they derived great pleasure every step of the way.

When the storyboard and exposure sheets had been completed, they were passed on to the layout artist, the cartoon's set designer, whose job was to create the bowling alley or golf course or living-room.

This timing sheet shows instructions for the cameraman in the righthand column, including moving the background (B.G.) on its traveling pegs.

A charming example of an exterior background. Notice the detail, complete down to the Christmas lights on the shrubbery. Note, too, how light from the front door window spills onto the little front step.

Backgrounds do much to enhance the storyline. Here we learn of "The Great Mousini." The tattered poster tells us that he is a great escape artist, without the need for a word of spoken dialogue.

THE GREAT
MOUSINI....

ESCAPE ARTIST
THE MOUSE NO TRAP
CAN HOLD

september 12

THE
GREAT
MOUSINI

MOUSINI

And here, with Mousini's name in lights, we see that his fame is indeed great. Background visuals were utilized as one of several ways to get around the fact that Tom and Jerry don't talk.

An interior background from the classic Baby Puss. *The bathroom is perfectly proportioned to little Jerry, while Tom appears, giant-sized, at the window like Alice in the white rabbit's garden.*

Many of the layouts were done by Richard Bickenbach, a master craftsman with a genius for design and an exquisite attention to detail.

The elegant dollhouse bathroom in *Baby Puss*, with its pedestal sink, tiny towel hanging neatly on the rail, carefully polished checkerboard tile floor, and tub with a duck's head for a faucet, is a charming example of time, talent and imagination lavishly and lovingly expended.

The layout artist also had to make sure that the dimensions of his set were in keeping with his characters' size – that the lamp in Jerry's mousehole bedroom is properly mouse-sized, while the lamp in the living-room must be scaled for human beings.

The layout artist also mapped out where the characters would move within his sets. Using the storyboard and exposure sheets as guides, he incorporated camera angles and pans (the camera scanning a long panorama) to determine whether a single drawing of a corner of the living-room would be necessary or a long vista of the entire room. He also maintained continuity of the various sets, or backgrounds, which averaged about 75 per cartoon.

When the layouts had been completed, the animators began their work. Tom & Jerry had four main animators, Irv Spence, Ray Patterson, Ken Muse and Ed Barge, all of whom might be assigned different sections of the same cartoon.

The Animator

"Bill would call me in," recalls Irv Spence, " and I would pick up 100 to 150 feet of animation layout and exposure sheets.

"He would go over the whole sequence, 150 feet, that's six weeks of work – we averaged 25 feet a week – and that was tough because they wanted super stuff."

How they got the super stuff was by a careful review of all the material – storyboards, exposure sheets, layouts – with Hanna not only explaining the specific actions, accents, and expressions for each character, but physically acting them out.

Spence recalls, "Bill could really get the expressions on Tom and Jerry and my gosh, you knew what they wanted after this little meeting.

"Now that's another thing; he would give me 150 feet knowing what I could do and I would know

Model sheets for the famous duo (below and on opposite page) show how they are developed from basic shapes, give scale between cat and mouse and display characteristic poses.

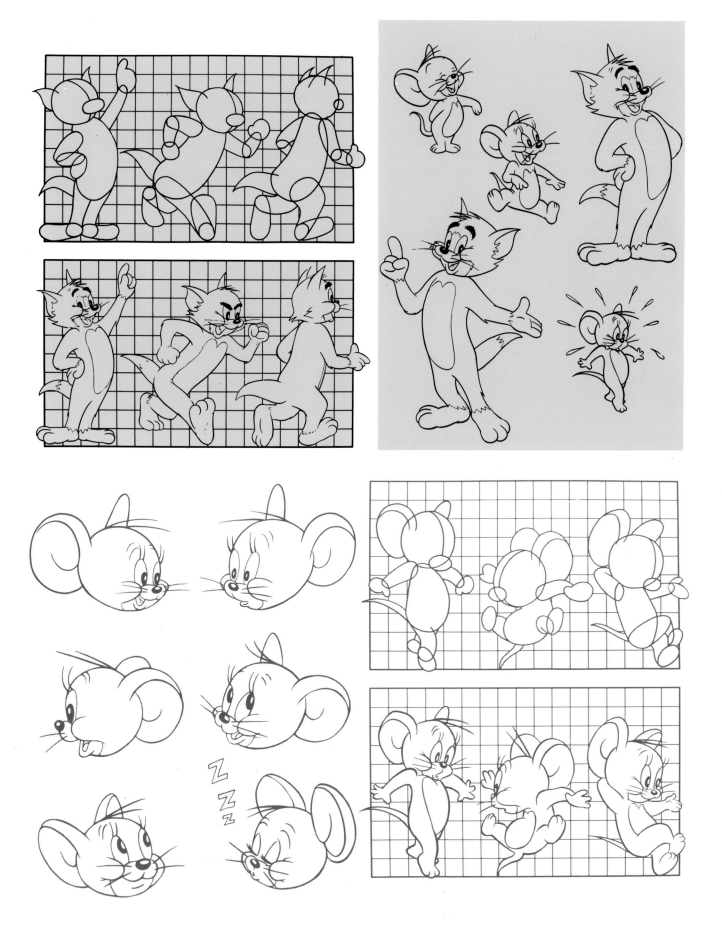

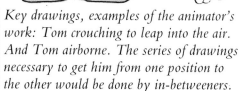

Key drawings, examples of the animator's work: Tom crouching to leap into the air. And Tom airborne. The series of drawings necessary to get him from one position to the other would be done by in-betweeners.

how to goof it up and exaggerate it and give him what he wanted."

Spence and his fellow animators "goofed up" the key drawings, bringing the thumbnail sketches from the storyboard to life. They executed the high points of every scene or gag – first Tom sticking his paw in a mousetrap and then Tom leaping in the air with pain, rage, and frustration.

"I like action," says Spence. "That's what they wanted on Tom. He had a lot of gusto. He'd run around the house, going about 90 miles an hour; he would run right around the walls. Then he'd race right back, really ready to go and cause some trouble."

The rough version of Tom enjoying a snooze. The cryptic note "truck out" in the righthand corner refers to a camera move which makes the subject appear to move further away (the same as a "zoom" in live-action movie making). The TV screen type frames around the drawing indicate the field, or camera area. Below it is a cel from the finished cartoon, Invasion of the Mouse Snatchers.

Of "little Jerry," he continues, "some of his acting . . . he was a little difficult because he was so small. He was fun to do, though, because of his personality."

The animator himself was an actor as well as an artist, communicating subtle (or more often) bold nuances of thought and emotion through the drawn characters. Tom and Jerry, without speaking a word, clearly express every idea that passes through their heads.

This is achieved not only through facial expression, but through movement. Jerry's swagger as he marches along the sideboard with a martini glass in *Puss Gets the Boot* tells everything one needs to know about how smug he feels. When Tom slinks away after breaking the flower pot and its stand, he is moving exactly the way every household cat slinks away in disgrace at some point in every domestic life.

Mammy's actions, too, clearly express her own personality. Her lumbering, heavy-footed gait is as clearly "Mammy" as the effervescent dash is "Jerry." This contributed much to the charm of the

Tom & Jerry cartoons, the animator's clear understanding of the mechanics of movement in animals and people, and his ability to act this out through his drawings.

Since the animator was acting while drawing, inventing little bits of business to accent the characters, creating mood and mayhem, his sketches reflected the rough, spontaneous mode in which they were made.

His assistant took these rough sketches and cleaned them up, tracing carefully over them with a black pencil, ironing out the kinks and smoothing out jagged edges, yet taking care to retain the integrity of the animator's original work. Even altering the width of a pencil line could change the expression of a subtle smile.

Then in-betweeners, usually apprentice or beginner animators, made all the drawings necessary to fill in the lengthy series of frames between the master animator's key sketches.

Animators, assistants and in-betweeners did their drawings on special tables fitted with a backlit sheet of glass with calibration pegs along one side. The drawing paper, of thin bond so that several sheets could be placed atop each other and viewed simultaneously, was punched to conform to the pegs on the table. Background, layout, ink and paint people, camera department, all had the same pegs to keep everything in register, or in the same position.

When the entire sequence of drawings – animator's, assistant's, and in-betweeners' – was finished, the animator flipped through the stack of sketches,

Animator's sketches. Although the drawings are rough, they sing with movement and expression. The righthand sketch of Jerry and the bottom sketch of Tom are in the process of clean-up. The animator has used a blue pencil while his assistant has refined it with black.

checking for smoothness of movement and intended expression.

At this point he might add drawings or make subtle changes to enhance the end result. Sometimes it was a matter of only five or six sketches, sometimes more, but this extra effort is part of what made Tom and Jerry magic.

Now the footage was pencil tested. The drawings, still in pencil sketch form without ink or paint, were photographed on 35mm motion picture film and spliced into a loop which could be run continuously through a movieola (a film editing machine).

To the uninitiated, a pencil test appears much the same as an amoeba swimming under a microscope lens, a vaguely connected series of squiggles wavering across the backlit viewing screen. The characters in a pencil test have form, but no color and no backgrounds on which to perform. To the animator, however, the pencil test is the first chance to see his creations in action, to observe how they move in the reality of the filmstrip as compared to

Three terrific sketches of Tom in mid-pursuit. The difference between pencil colors? As Lefty Callahan explains, "Sometimes I like this red pencil and sometimes it just doesn't work for me."

the planning stages of pencil and paper.

Here, hunched over the tiny viewing screen, the animator again reviewed his work and made any changes he deemed necessary.

The revised sequence was then rephotographed, and meeting the animator's final approval, sent on to the screening room. This was a theater, not a public one with paying audiences and popcorn, but a viewing room in the Cartoon Department where the newborn sequence was aired before its originators.

Bill and Joe, often accompanied by all the Tom & Jerry animators, watched the pencil test, which they had envisioned but thus far seen only as storyboard and exposure sheet, unfold. This was the first payoff for the animator, the opportunity to see the fruits of his labors warmly received by an audience.

Occasionally, Hanna and Barbera requested additional changes and these were made and the resulting sequence once again polished up, reviewed, and screened.

A finished cel from the same scene as the sketches above retains the rhythm and vitality intended by the animator.

Coloring It In

Having passed final muster, the sequence went on to the ink and paint department. Here the background man put the finishing touches on the layout artist's "sets," coloring in and lending texture to walls, carpets or rolling fields of grass, sprinkling a garden with spring flowers or a night sky with a myriad shimmering stars.

Here, too, a legion of inkers and painters put the pencil sketches into final form. Wearing white gloves to avoid getting finger smudges or oils on their work surfaces, inkers painstakingly traced each drawing in black india ink on a sheet of clear celluloid, called a "cel."

The hand drawn cels then passed on to the painters, who, as their title suggests, painted each cel, meticulously, one by one, in a kind of animation department paint by numbers kit. Color model girls, working with the background artist and Bill Hanna, had already made up a chart detailing which colors were to be used for each character and object in the cartoon. Care had to be taken to ensure that the gray of Tom's coat, for example, did not match

Four poses from an action sequence leave no doubt that Tom has a problem. Many cels will be required to complete the sequence. Top and below right are two such cels.

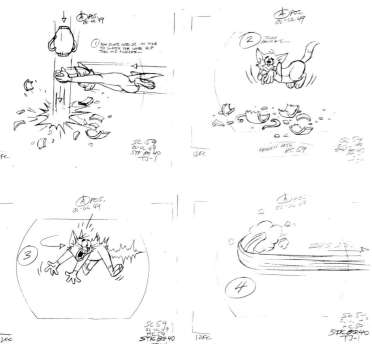

too closely the gray of castle walls, therefore rendering Tom invisible in comparison.

Costumes were keyed, or color chosen, as carefully as for any live action actors. Tom's orange and green striped suit in *The Zoot Cat*, Jerry's and Tuffy's blue uniforms in *The Two Mouseketeers*, Mammy's ubiquitous stockings, all were considered both as definition of the character and as a part of the whole.

Painting in the cels sounds easy, but was an art in itself. Of prime importance is what any child knows, that the artist must stay "within the lines." This was achieved not only by steady hands, but with a bit of cheating. Cels were inked on the front and painted on the back. Because the ink lines were fairly thick, the artist allowed her paint to flow just halfway into the line, so that a smooth, uninterrupted color appeared when the cel was turned rightside up.

Painting on the back of the cel also ensured that brush strokes and puddling didn't show on the front, the side the camera, and the audience, sees.

In *The Bodyguard*, Tom paints up a gumball to resemble cheese with which to tempt Jerry in a matter of seconds, but painting the scheming cat took far longer, and far more patience.

When one considers that the average cartoon used 12,000 different cels, it's a wonder that more than one was made in a year. Yet Hanna, Barbera, and their staff turned out half a dozen or more a year.

And, according to them all, the pace was leisurely. "More fun," says Joe Barbera, "than working."

Whether they considered it work or not, the cartoon was being made. While animation, layouts, clean up, inking and painting were being done, the musical director was preparing his part of the film.

Music, Maestro

Music played an extremely important role in the Tom & Jerry series; it helped describe what the cat and mouse could not say verbally, set the mood from the opening credits on, carried out the theme, and reinforced the timing laid out by Bill Hanna.

Scott Bradley, a diminutive genius with a shock of blond hair, was the sole musical director for Tom & Jerry, as well as a host of other MGM cartoon stars.

Before the fall, Tom juggling dishes. This is a background with the character cel placed over it. The very next frame, showing minute changes. Tom's eyes have lowered and all the crockery has shifted slightly, harbinger of the catastrophe to come.

Jerry finds a dance partner in New Mouse in the House, *a made for television Filmation cartoon. At top left is a preliminary sketch and at right and below are finished cels, showing what the mechanical cutie does with him.*

Tom ties cherries to a tree – a preliminary sketch. Notice that in this later date Filmation cartoon, Invasion of the Mouse Snatchers, *xeroxing has been called into play. Below is a finished cel from the same scene.*

Above: *Animator's sketch of Tom and Jerry, with an unfortunate feathered friend. Note that Bertram, like every character in a cartoon, has his own model sheet.* Below: *A finished cel from the same scene.*

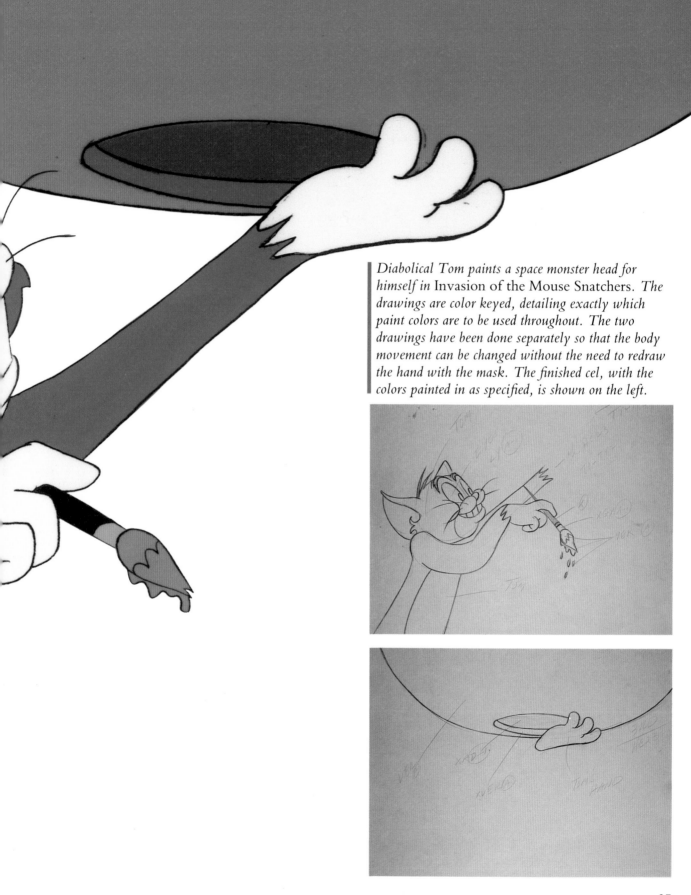

Diabolical Tom paints a space monster head for himself in Invasion of the Mouse Snatchers. *The drawings are color keyed, detailing exactly which paint colors are to be used throughout. The two drawings have been done separately so that the body movement can be changed without the need to redraw the hand with the mask. The finished cel, with the colors painted in as specified, is shown on the left.*

A painted cel (and curtain backdrop) from the front, with ink lines clearly visible. Today, "ink" lines are achieved by simply xeroxing the cleaned-up drawing onto a blank cel. In the Golden Age of animation, they were hand inked. And the same cel from the back, showing brush strokes and paint build-up.

A composer as well as director of the Cartoon Department orchestra, Bradley was creative in his use of music and melody.

In *Dr. Jekyll and Mr. Mouse*, Tom brews up a hellish concoction of milky white household chemicals with which to permanently remove the milk craving Jerry. The house is dark and eerie, and Tom's shadow looms ominously out of the walls. Bradley rounded out the illustration of gothic horror with a sinister mix of English horn, bass clarinet and viola.

Sometimes his work was more sprightly. When Nibbles, Jerry's junior cohort, scurries joyfully across the banquet table toward a mouthwatering tower of cheese in *The Two Mouseketeers*, his happy romp is playfully underscored by a quick, romping passage on the piano.

Besides scoring his own music, Bradley freely used current MGM hit songs and old favorites to illustrate Tom and Jerry's antics. "The Trolley Song" from the popular Judy Garland film, *Meet Me in St. Louis* was used in *Cat Fishin'* to highlight the unsuspecting Tom reeling in Spike rather than a fish, and in *Old Rockin' Chair Tom* as the pacing for a story of Tom & Jerry up against a rival for cat of the house honors.

Both the U.S. Navy theme song, "Anchors Aweigh" and the popular tune, "Darktown Strutters Ball" were used in *The Mouse Comes to Dinner*; and the rousing finish to *The Yankee Doodle Mouse*, with Lt Jerry Mouse's triumph and the American flag, is climaxed by "Hooray for the Red, White and Blue."

Lyrics were used as well as music on occasion. Tom romances his girlfriend, Toots, with "Is You Is or Is You Ain't My Baby?" in *Solid Serenade* and

A music sheet for scenes 54 through 57 of Tee for Two. *The page also notes the action taking place and a variety of bams, plops and glugs – sound effects of the best sort.*

attempts to woo her by crooning (courtesy of a phonograph) a cowboy tune in *Texas Tom*.

And of course, the Oscar winning *The Cat Concerto* and *Johann Mouse* used wonderfully melodic orchestral arrangements.

The MGM cartoon orchestra consisted originally of between 16 and 30 musicians, although in later years this core group could expand to 45 men when a particular score required a larger ensemble.

Before the orchestra could even rehearse its stuff, however, the score had to be written. And this was done before the cartoon had even been pencil tested. Scott Bradley wrote, arranged, cut and pasted his original melodies and borrowed tunes without seeing a single cel.

This was the beauty of the exposure sheet. Since it was already mapped out frame by frame, the tempo had already been set. Bradley could write his music using the beats designated by Bill Hanna. (One, two, three frames for Jerry scurrying would be a quick glissando on the piano; one, two, three, four . . . eleven, twelve frames for Tom's shadow looming on the wall would be a long, slow measure for the viola).

Tom and Jerry did more with music than moving about with it in the background. They danced to music. Jerry was a particularly fine dancer, using as a partner everything from a drapery tassel to Tom's fingers (*Johann Mouse*) to a banana peel (*Muscle Beach Tom*). He waltzes, cha-chas, polkas, and even ice skates (*Mouse In Manhattan* and *Mice Follies*).

When one understands the exposure sheet, it is easy to see how little Jerry swoops with Fred Astaire

Jerry, in his country mouse hat, ice skates on a centerpiece mirror with a placecard doll in Mouse In Manhattan. *The details in this little scene are superb: the cut glass vase in the foreground, the chair back forming a sort of bandstand shell, the night-lit city skyline. Notice, too, how Jerry's fingers are extended in proper dancing style and how the doll's eyes look off and away.*

agility across the floor (or table, as the case may be). The one, two, three tempo of his run is as much a description of the timing sheet as of a choreographer's chart.

And in fact, Jerry has been choreographed with the best. As a lonely little monarch in the live action film *Anchors Aweigh*, he dances with Gene Kelly, matching his human partner's moves step for step. In an enchanting sequence, the two glide across the throne room floor as smoothly as if they had rehearsed for years. In truth, they never met once during filming.

Kelly devised the dance and then performed it on film, in the first step of a matte process (a technique where the only background is a steady backlit blue). The Cartoon Department took this piece of film and rotoscoped it, meaning that they traced each frame of Gene's dance, just as if he were a cartoon character, onto paper, which gave them the blueprint for Jerry's mirror movements. They then drew Jerry's dance, frame by frame.

Jerry's performance was filmed on a blue matte background and the two pieces of film combined. It now appeared that Gene and Jerry were dancing together, side by side.

Using a similar process, Jerry, this time joined by Tom, swam with Esther Williams in *Dangerous When Wet*. Wearing swim fins and bemused expressions (for even a cat and mouse think it odd to find themselves underwater), they follow Esther's lovely moves in a dreamy, watery musical sequence.

To ensure that every beat of music used the same number of frames, the score was written while a metronomic beat clicked off the tempo; during recording, the orchestra members all wore earphones into which intoned this same click. In the finished cartoon, actions and music flowed together in perfect sync.

Dialogue and sound effects were also recorded while the cartoon was still on the animator's drawing board.

Tom and Jerry cavort with Gene Kelly in Anchors Aweigh. *Because a live action/animation sequence like this had never been attempted before, Kelly went to Walt Disney for advice. The creator of the "other mouse" heartily concurred with the project's feasibility but was too busy to take it on himself, so Hanna and Barbera were called upon — with wonderful results. This photograph is a publicity shot for the film — although Tom had a brief part, as Jerry's valet, he never danced with Kelly.*

Jerry the Mouse King with Gene the sailor. Dancing and singing are forbidden in the kingdom because Jerry himself can't sing or dance. But after a quick lesson from Gene, "Look at me!" the little monarch proudly exclaims. "I'm dancing!"

In Dangerous When Wet, *Esther Williams has fallen asleep and dreamed her way into an underwater cartoon adventure with Tom and Jerry. Here she dives into the scene, her real bubbles quickly turning to animated ones. A publicity still, this particular frame doesn't appear in the film.*

Although Tom and Jerry don't talk, other characters do. Mammy talks – a lot, usually threatening the always goldbricking Tom, therefore setting the pace for the ensuing action. Spike talks, in the gruff, tough tones of a longshoreman or fight manager. Nibbles' tiny, enchanting voice pipes out *les bons mots* in French, and various other characters, from guard captains to ungainly ducklings, also have speaking parts on occasion. Sometimes it seems that everyone in Tom and Jerry's world talks but the stars themselves. (On rare occasions they, too, speak a line or two, perhaps surprising themselves as much as the audience.)

The characters were given voice, their mouths moving in sync with their words, also courtesy of the exposure sheet, which spelled out exactly how many frames would be used per word of dialogue.

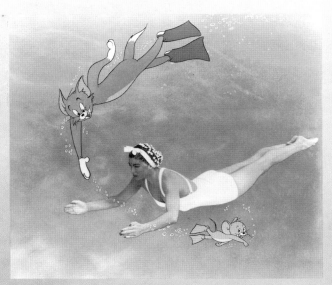

Here, Esther gets acquainted with the cat and mouse. Then, forgetting she's supposed to swim the English Channel, she mimics a passing turtle, but Tom and Jerry soon set her back on course. In the publicity still at bottom right, the prop man has goofed – Tom and Jerry aren't wearing their flippers.

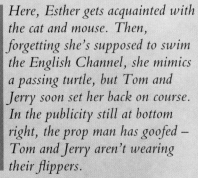

Crash, Boom and Bang

Tom and Jerry could do without dialogue, but their films would not be complete without sound effects. Their endless battles were richly punctuated with slams, bangs, screeches, yowls, thuds, thunks, and other noises that defy description.

In *Texas Tom*, Tom the cowhand, in a kerchief and ten-gallon hat, is sitting on the porch playing with a rope which he makes into a lasso to snare Jerry, garbed in his own kerchief and a tiny ten-quart hat.

First we hear a *whsst* as the rope is flung to chase Jerry along the side of the bunkhouse. Jerry rounds the corner with a *screech*, the rope in hot pursuit. But the rope catches him and he rebounds with a lovely *boiing* in midair and a distinctive thump as he hits the ground.

While Tom is reeling him in, Jerry gets snagged by a spur, which makes a *pling* sound. Two tiny thuds as he hits the ground again, a *thump* as he is reeled onto an inconvenient board, a *thud/bang* as he hits the board, an *"aiiyyy"* from Jerry as he lights on an even more inconvenient cactus, a rubbery balloony sound as Tom pulls him off the spines, and then a satisfying *blam* as he slaps Tom in the face with the cactus.

All these sound effects – *whsst, screech, boiing, thump, pling, thud, thud, thump, thud/bang, "aiiyyy," blam* – which used only about 15 seconds of screen time, were detailed on an exposure sheet and recorded prior to the completion of the cartoon.

While the art work is in progress, Jim Faris, sound effects technician, combs his file of sound track clippings for something to fit the archery scene. Note the interesting array of other noises at his disposal, such as "whaps - plops," "hits – slaps," "footsteps," and "explosions."

Left: *Animator Irv Spence looks for just the right expression for Tom's face.*

Below left: *Producer Fred Quimby watches Bill Hanna and Joe Barbera act out a bit of business from* Two Little Indians. *The cartoon's storyboard is on the wall behind them.*

Below right: *As the studio caption for this photo explained, "Layout man Richard Bickenbach is a combination art director and set decorator. Part of his job is to plan and sketch the various backgrounds used in the cartoon . . . in this case an adobe wall. He is shown here with Midge Sterges, the cue sheet girl (equivalent to the script supervisor on a live action picture)." Note the animation table with its circular cutout and the model sheets pinned to the wall in front of him.*

Putting It All Together

When the soundtrack of dialogue and effects had been recorded, the music scored and recorded, the cels animated, inked and painted, backgrounds designed and colored, it was time to complete the spell, to magically forge all the disparate elements into one; to make the two dimensional beings come to life in a well-rounded world of their own.

The camera room was where this final bit of sorcery took place. Here the cels and background were painstakingly photographed within the cleanliness of a hospital surgery. Any speck of dust or dirt would loom up the size of a small moon on the screen.

The background, which had been painted in watercolors on a sheet of thick paper, was set into registration on the camera stand's special pegs. Then, to use the earlier example of the three different cels with Spike sleeping, Jerry scampering and Tom stalking, the three cels were placed one

One of "a staff of female inkers" (as the original studio caption put it) traces a drawing onto a cel.

In-betweeners at work. The man in the foreground is working on a drawing for Two Little Indians.

46

above the other on top of the background, and flattened with a sheet of glass. This presented a complete picture – dog, cat and mouse in action on the living-room background.

The background, set on traveling peg bars, could be moved beneath a stationary character cel, thus giving the illusion of a figure traveling across the room.

The background did not always move; sometimes the living-room remained in place while the characters moved within a given area.

The area, or field, which the camera photographed was 8¾in. by 12in. The camera was a regular motion picture camera, except that it was stopped after each frame so the cels and/or background could be changed.

Right: *The paint department with its storehouse of water colors and brushes.*

Opposite: *Painter Brooke Mitchell carefully fills in the colors on cels which have been traced by the inkers. She is shown here doing water color brush work on a canvas backed garden chair which is the main prop in a* Two Little Indians *scene.*

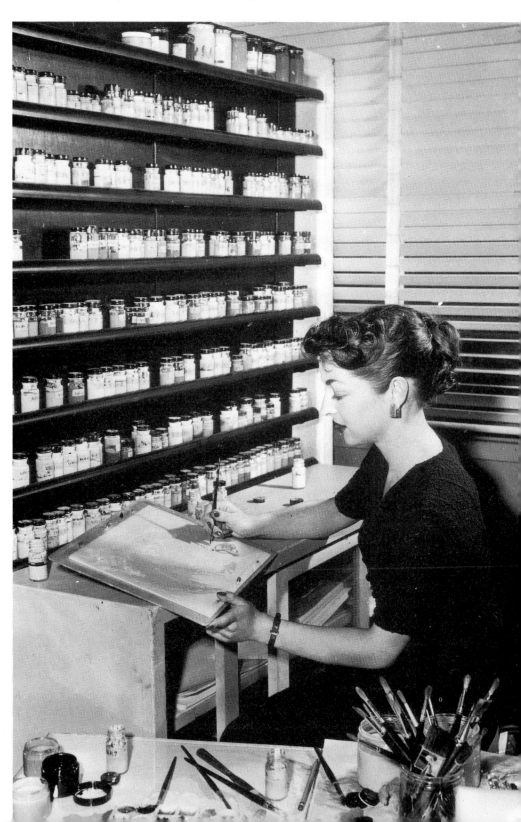

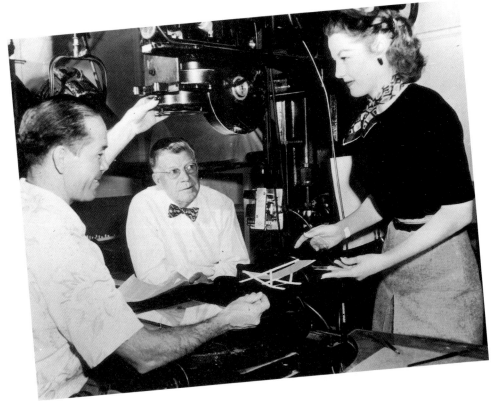

Cameraman Jack Stevenson receives the canvas chair cel from Brooke Mitchell and, with Fred Quimby supervising, is ready to photograph the completed set-up. Over the adobe wall background, which is drawn on heavy paper, he places three of the transparent cels – one of Tom, another of Jerry, and the third of the chair – secures them in perfect register under a glass plate, and clicks the camera shutter.

This is the set-up as recorded by the camera. In their perennial war of cat and mouse, Jerry has momentarily turned the tables and is attacking with lighted kitchen matches as his flaming arrows. Note that this is the same scene acted out by Hanna and Barbera for Fred Quimby.

The closing scene from Two
Little Indians, *as Jerry, his
orphan scouts, and a somewhat
battered Tom sit down to smoke
the peace pipe.*

49

RICH HOGAN at a story board pins up sketches.

JOE BARBERA and Bill Hanna created Tom and Jerry.

IRVING SPENCE makes cartoon characters move.

SCOTT BRADLEY'S music sells subtler nuances of comedy.

TEX AVERY, l., draws Sammy Skunk as Otto Englander, at center, works out story sequence, and William Hanna, right, demonstrates a bit of action for Tom, the cat in new Tom and Jerry cartoon. Men are pictured above at a story meeting with Fred Quimby, center, boss of MGM short subject production.

"When and if you ever get to California and go to see the MGM studio," went the text for this MGM Distributor magazine article, *"set aside some of your time to visit the Cartoon Studio, one of the most interesting places you'll ever see!"* Tex Avery, famous for creating Droopy Dog and the Wolf and the Girl, and story man Otto Englander, were not part of the Tom & Jerry unit. They were apparently included here for the purpose of the article.

50

Finally, every cel had been photographed in exact order, just as on the exposure sheet; all the camera work was done, resulting in a single strip of film. Now this was combined with the sound effects/dialogue and music score, both of which had been recorded on pictureless filmstrips, with only the soundtrack along one edge, and both of which were the exact length as the photographed filmstrip. When combined, these three strips formed the release print which was sent to movie theaters and audiences anxiously anticipating the next installment of Tom and Jerry's antics.

Hanna, Barbera and their staff derived as much enjoyment from the cat and mouse as did their audiences.

"A good animator puts life and believability in a character; he brings him alive and you think of him not as a cartoon character but as a human," says Bill Hanna.

"I guess it's almost childlike when you stop to analyze it. An adult man is thinking of a cartoon character and there is something emotional in the scene. You react with feeling. I have seen cartoons, and tears come to my eyes.

"I've even talked material like that and choke up when I try to tell it. It's just, I think, the way you involve yourself in the character, or feel for it."

Producer Hugh Harman, left, and cameraman Jack Stevens.

Producer Rudolph Ising, right, and W. D. Burness, animator.

4. Background artist Joe Smith paints separate backgrounds which seldom need to be redrawn for each character movement.

5. The girls in the inking department clearly outline the character sketches as they come to them from the animators.

6. Jean Higgins, color artist, selects the proper colors to suit the character and mood of any particular scene or situation.

7. The girls in the painting department fill in the colors in the next operation before the drawings are ready for filming.

8. Music plays an important part in all M-G-M cartoons. Director Scott Bradley synchronizes it with the action in the film.

9. Important too is sound technician and special effects man P. McAlpin who supplies sound interpretations of the action.

Fred C. Quimby, right, head of the Cartoon Department and the man largely responsible for M-G-M being the first major producer to make its own cartoons, is shown above with C. G. Maxwell, production supervisor.

The M-G-M Cartoon Building, housing more than 150 artists and technicians who produce 18 cartoons in Technicolor annually.

MEN
WHO MAKE
SHORTS

MGM

CARTOON DEPARTMENT...

1. After a story has been written the first step in making an animated cartoon is the sketching of the characters. Robert Allen uses live models.

2. Co-directors Joe Barbera and William Hanna develop the character to its full humorous possibilities, suggest expressions and tricks to humanize it.

3. Animator Lovell Norman draws the characters in many consecutive motions which, when filmed and run off, give them "life".

Two pages from a studio publication show how cartoons are made. In photo number two, a very young Hanna and Barbera are hard at work on Puss Gets the Boot.

51

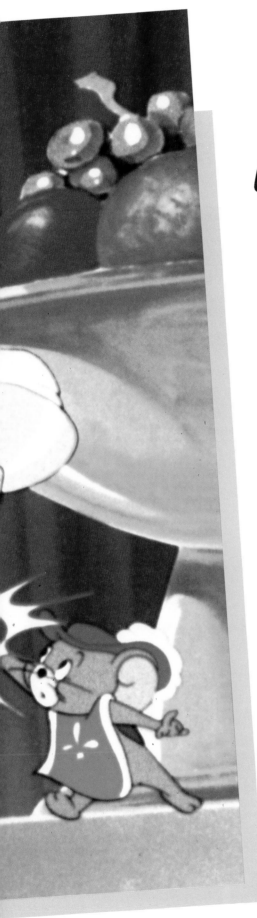

MOVIE STAR MOUSE AND CAT

ithin the Tom & Jerry cartoon building, not all the gags were drawn on paper. Being a gagster with a pencil often meant being a gagster in reality as well. But where Tom and Jerry used firecrackers and sticks of dynamite, the cartoonists used less explosive devices.

The projection room, dark and with the only telephone, should have had "Enter At Your Own Risk" written in neon over the door, for often when you threw on the light switch all hell broke loose. The unwary would come away with bright red ears from lipstick smeared on the telephone earpiece or frazzled nerves from music blasting out of a phonograph while 1,000 watts of light suddenly slashed the dark and blizzards of paper blew before a very strong fan.

The perpetrators of much of this madness were Irv Spence and his assistant, Oliver "Lefty" Callahan.

Their office was next door to Hanna and Barbera's office, and the only thing standing between Irv's desk and Joe's was a wall. On one memorable occasion, while Spence was away at

lunch, Joe drilled a hole through the wall, which would be level with Irv's face when he sat down to work.

Lunch hour came and went. Joe, peering expectantly through the hole, saw Spence return to his office, sit down at his desk, and begin to draw. Having got his victim in his sights, Joe filled his mouth with water, placed a straw through the hole, and splat, Spence suddenly found himself with water cascading down his face, not unlike a scene in *The Mouse Comes to Dinner*, in which Jerry takes soup in his mouth and squirts it in Tom's face.

In the cartoonists' world, as in the cartoon world of Tom & Jerry, one gag is always the prelude to a bigger and better one, and Spence immediately set to work devising something devious.

He came up with an elaborate contraption that would, providing it worked, reward its inventor with a larger payoff and the last laugh.

The key to his invention was that above Joe's

In A Mouse in the House, *Tom and his rival, Butch, each thinking the other is disguised as the housekeeper, have given her a good paddling. Here they begin to realize their mistake. Mammy was voiced to perfection by Lillian Randolph.*

Fed up with being forced to blow on the soup to cool it, Jerry has filled his mouth with the hot broth and is about to spring it on Tom in The Mouse Comes to Dinner.

desk, and consequently right above his head, was a light fixture, activated by a switch that also turned on a fan.

While Joe was away from his office, Spence filled a film can lid with water. Then he tied one end of a string to a ruler and the other end to the fan near the light fixture. The ruler was set under the lid, ruler and lid carefully balanced on the light fixture, and the whole contraption rigged strategically just over the desk. When the light, and fan, were flicked on, the revolution of the fan would wind up the string, pull the ruler out from under the lid, and the lid would fall down and douse Joe with water.

Spence fairly danced out of Joe's office, grinning with anticipation, and trotted back to his own office on the other side of the wall. Waiting with the same diabolical glee as Tom when he sets a snare for Jerry, he listened for Joe's footsteps. Soon he heard them, coming up the stairs, along the hall, and into the room. Then came the sound of the fan starting. He pictured the string winding tighter and tighter. Suddenly there was a crash. It worked!

Spence darted a glance out; like all good pranksters he was dying to see the results of his labor.

But Joe, like Jerry mouse, was quick on his feet. He had heard a rattling above his head and jumped out of the way just as the water splashed down. Instead of a drenching, he got only a few drops.

In addition to, or in spite of, the practical jokes, the Cartoon Division was a magical place to work. A few minutes walk would take you to the sidewalks of New York or the streets of Paris via the MGM back lot. Sitting in the California sun, the cartoonists ate their brown bag lunches in Atlanta one day and El Paso the next.

Rubbing Shoulders with the Stars

Once a week they splurged with lunch at the commissary, where the movie stars dined. The cartoonists, in their pencil-smudged shirtsleeves, sat at their little table, admiring the costumed actors in their on-set finery. The ladies, adorned in silks and satins, sat scattered about like jeweled peacocks at a

The Million Dollar Cat *has Tom and Jerry living the high life with inherited money.* Top: *They relax in a limo on the way to their ritzy Park Avenue penthouse.* Below: *Jerry makes life difficult for Tom, who can't fight back due to the stipulations of the will.*

fancy dress party while the men all occupied one big table in the center of the room. Clark Gable, in the ruffled shirt and white tie of Rhett Butler, Leslie Howard in a satin lined cloak, Spencer Tracy, Robert Young, attired in the poshest of outfits, gambled at the end of the meal to see who would pick up the tab.

On quieter days, the cartoonists took sandwiches out to the back lot lake and engaged in a little illegal carp fishing. The lake was used for exterior scenes, the carp to keep it clean. But they were nice, fat, old carp and irresistible to animators.

Using bits of sandwich and hooks with the barbs filed off, the cartoonists, in the spirit of *Cat Fishin'* Tom and Jerry, cast their lines, and before

Tom and Jerry in a publicity still
for the Mouseketeers series (there
were four: The Two
Mouseketeers, Touche, Pussy
Cat, Tom and Cherie, and
Royal Cat Nap).

the bread dissolved, had usually managed to reel one in. They also sailed little model boats on the lake and lazed in the sun. And on the way back to the cartoon building, they stopped at various soundstages, watching in fascination as stars like Katharine Hepburn and Greta Garbo enacted elegant scenes. In the words of Lefty Callahan, "I don't think there was anyplace like it."

The proximity to the main lot, where creative genius permeated the air, the pranks and fishing and picnics, paid off, for Tom and Jerry, and through them, their creators, won seven Academy Awards.

Oscar, in all his golden glory, was given to Tom & Jerry for the following films:

> THE YANKEE DOODLE MOUSE 1943
> MOUSE TROUBLE 1944
> QUIET PLEASE 1945
> THE CAT CONCERTO 1946
> THE LITTLE ORPHAN 1948
> THE TWO MOUSEKETEERS 1951
> JOHANN MOUSE 1952

These cartoons were selected by the Academy of Motion Picture Arts and Sciences from among the best Hollywood had to offer, including that tough Disney competitor, Mickey Mouse, and Warner Brothers top looney tuners, Bugs and Porky.

But even before this, they had to undergo stiff competition from their own studio. Each December Fred Quimby, MGM's Cartoon Department producer, and his assistants chose four or five films which they felt were the cream of their crop for that year. These were then submitted to a jury of 60 studio executives, live-action producers and directors. They cast ballots for the "best" cartoon and that one was submitted to the Academy.

Taking a closer look, that they were chosen by both studio and Academy is no wonder. One must marvel anew on each viewing at the freshness of the storylines, the sharpness of the timing, and the brilliance of the animators' craftsmanship.

When Jerry tries to push a grandfather clock to the floor in Quiet Please, for example, his entire body becomes involved in the work of shoving over such a heavy piece – sitting in the audience we can feel the tremendous strain on his tiny mouse muscles. And this, as much as the novel situation of mouse baiting cat, provokes the laugh when he finally achieves his goal – we know how hard he's worked and feel just as perkily superior as he does.

In *The Little Orphan*, when Nibbles swallows an orange whole and Jerry whacks it out of him with a knife, it's not just another mindless cartoon smack. Tom & Jerry's animators took the time to think out each situation and let the character act accordingly. The look of astonishment on Nibbles' face as the orange shoots out of him is pure joy to watch, and again provokes a laugh for its own sake, quite apart from the cat-mouse chase to come.

Whether one watches these cartoons on the big screen, at the theater, or at home on the video recorder (sometimes even more fun, for the amazement that comes with putting on the freeze frame and noticing how incredibly smooth the animation is, frame by frame), these Oscar winners are, like the Thanksgiving feast little Nibbles is after, totally delectable.

A pencil sketch from The Milky Waif, *in which Nibbles makes his first appearance, copied from xeroxed material.*

This cartoon recast the contemporary war between the Allied and Axis powers in decidedly rodent/feline terms. Set in the cellar of a stolidly suburban house, it captured the rousing emotions of a battle squarely fought and roundly won, as well as the first Academy Award for the dueling pair.

With Jerry in a bottlecap hat and Tom in a succession of homemade helmets, featuring bunkers, barricades, an inventive bomber and an even more inventive parachute, *The Yankee Doodle Mouse* uses all the conventional trappings of war to tell the story of a most unconventional battle.

From the opening scene, a "Cat Raid Shelter" sign tacked to a kitchen stool, we know we are in the midst of a battle zone.

Jerry rushes past the sign, Tom in hot pursuit, through the kitchen and down the cellar steps, where two more signs point toward the shelter.

"This is it!" proclaims a sign over the mouse-hole shelter, which has been sandbagged with old books. Tom plants himself, catlike, in front of the hole, peering frustratedly in. Jerry uses a mousetrap as a tomato launcher and fires through the door into Tom's face. The battle has begun.

Jerry scurries up the inside of the wall and out onto a shelf on which is a box of hen-grenades, or, as the uninitiated might call them, eggs. Grabbing one in each hand, he lobs them at Tom, and then whistles. Tom, wiping tomato off his face, looks up and promptly gets two eggs in the face.

Running for cover behind a barrel, he peeks around only to receive another egg in the eye, the broken shell forming a monocle and the dripping yolk its golden chain.

Jerry, meanwhile, has skidded around onto a case of champagne and shoots off the corks which hit Tom, now wearing a pot for a helmet. Tom loses his balance and falls into a tub of water, landing in his pot. A gleeful Jerry now releases a brick resting on a bent-back spatula as a catapult, sinking both pot and passenger.

A Mouse Headquarters, Cheese Division, war communique appears on the screen: Sighted cat – sank same. Signed . . . Lt Jerry Mouse.

Back in his mousehole, peppered with signs (That friendly rat may tell a cat; and Shut your trap), Jerry, wearing a bottlecap on his head, peers through his plumbing pipe periscope. He scans the cellar, finally sighting the enemy sneaking up with a mallet.

Tom, mallet in readiness over his shoulder, places a scrap of cheese in front of the hole, but Jerry has seen him through the scope and races out of another mousehole past his waiting jeep (a cheese grater on a roller skate) inside the ironing board cupboard. Jerry pushes on the ironing board, forcing open the cupboard door, and the board slams down on the unsuspecting Tom.

Now Lt Mouse races down the ironing board in his jeep and comes out underneath the cat. Skidding around, he makes another pass and Tom gets grated again.

Two classic scenes from The Yankee Doodle Mouse. *Right: Tom's first assault after chasing Jerry into the cellar. After being tomatoed, egged, corked, sunk, grated, and paddled, he throws a firecracker at Jerry. Below: Jerry confuses Tom into thinking he wants the firecracker. Here, the cat has second thoughts.*

As Tom sits rubbing his tush, Jerry rides triumphantly past, raising his bottlecap helmet in the air in a smug salute. Too smug, for the jeep crashes into a bench leg, collapsing the bench and sending cans of food and a large sack of flour tumbling down about his ears.

But Jerry is quick. He grabs a corner of the conveniently torn sack and scampers around the room with flour billowing out behind him, making a wonderful smokescreen beneath which to hide, for it begins just over his head.

Tom now thunders into position but can see nothing through the flour smoke. Jerry wallops him repeatedly with a board. Poor Tom can't see where the attack is coming from. After the third smack, however, he lowers his head, finds Jerry – and Jerry hits him again.

Tom barricades himself behind a box, a bowl

Above: *Lt Mouse, shot down by the enemy, floats gently to earth in a very creative parachute, while moments later (below), Tom smugly watches his fireball detachment chase Jerry around the basement.*

on his head for a helmet this time. He throws a firecracker over the box at Jerry, who immediately tosses it back. The lit stick is handed off repeatedly until Tom, confusedly thinking he wants it, keeps it. Jerry hides a snicker and Tom gets the bang.

Jerry jumps into a teakettle. Tom throws a firecracker in, Jerry sneaks out through the spout, and Tom, waiting to hear the bang, opens the lid and sticks his head in, just in time to have it explode, putting him in blackface with a daisy petal frame.

Now Tom sends a firecracker via paper airplane. Jerry sees it coming and blows it back to him. The plane soars, circles around, slips right under

Tom and blows up beneath his chin, leaving him again with a charred face.

Jerry's turn. He plants a king-sized firecracker right behind Tom and scurries away. Tom sniffs the air, turns around, sees the firecracker, freezes. The firecracker splits in half, revealing a smaller one, which peels down to reveal a still smaller firecracker. This pops harmlessly open to reveal successively smaller ones, until finally all that is left is a tiny replica of the original. Tom picks it up, chuckles, and it explodes like the all mighty.

Jerry squeezes through a hole in a barrel and jumps into a Flying Tiger airplane fashioned from a box tied down with a garter. He releases the plane with its load of light bulb bombs and soars around the cellar until he sights his target. Having fired all the "bombs," he releases a banana torpedo.

Tom now grabs a firecracker cannon and begins shooting at Jerry's plane. He keeps missing because his eyes are closed most of the time. When he finally opens them his aim improves and he shoots down the plane.

But Lt Mouse, always prepared, floats gently to earth in a brassière parachute and runs for the safety of the mousehole.

Tom pursues, thrusting the cannon into the mousehole, knocking the plaster off the walls all around the room as the mortars follow Jerry.

These fireballs, with mysterious homing devices, chase Jerry around the cellar while Tom watches confidently from inside a barrel. They follow Jerry into a hose, which he then fires at Tom, exploding the barrel and turning it into a bicycle, which he rides until it hits the wall.

Tom fires a dart gun at Jerry, catching him by the tail and dangling him over the mousehole. He grabs him, dashes to a rocket, lights it, and begins tying Jerry to it.

But Jerry helpfully ties Tom's hands to it instead and Tom is catapulted into space where he and the rocket explode into fireworks and the American flag. To the tune of "Hooray for the Red White and Blue" and the sound of bursting fireworks, Jerry, chest puffed out proudly, salutes the flag.

Final war communique: Send more cats. Signed . . . Lt Jerry Mouse.

Above: *The enemy has captured Lt Mouse.* Below: *He ties him to a rocket. But Jerry soon turns the tables, sending the cat aloft and striking a blow for freedom fighters everywhere.*

MOUSE TROUBLE
1944

The brilliance of *Mouse Trouble* is its absolute simplicity. Based on the premise of a how-to book for would be mouse snatchers, the cartoon details the difficulties Tom gets into trying to follow its easy directions. What neither he nor the book has taken into account is that Jerry is not your average mouse, and that he has read the book as well.

The cartoon opens with a mailman delivering a package. Tom eagerly rushes to the mailbox, pulls out his package, and speeds back into the house in a blur. He excitedly rips off the wrapping to reveal a book – How To Catch A Mouse (A Random Mouse Book). He begins reading.

"Chapter I: First – Locate the Mouse. The mouse is usually found hiding in baseboards or pantrys . . . Sometimes he's much closer than you think . . . Be Alert." The mouse, right under Tom's nose, is reading right along with him but the cat is too absorbed in the text to notice. He finally sees him and tries to catch him in his paws, but Jerry slams the book on him and rushes into his hole.

"Chapter II: NEXT . . . Try the simple mouse trap." Tom baits the trap, dropping a feather on it to check the sensitivity. It works. Smiling broadly, he sets the trap before the hole. Jerry struggles to get the cheese morsel off the trap but can't budge it. He pries it, kicks it, climbs on and wrestles with it. Finally wrenching it free, he swallows it in one bite, and uses the trap as a springboard to dive back into his hole. Tom picks up the trap and it snaps on his finger.

"Chapter III: A Snare Trap never fails." A rope, tied to a tree branch, snaking through the open window, is set in a circle around a piece of cheese. Tom, obviously the perpetrator of this piece of mischief, sneaks away to await Jerry's arrival. But before he can turn around, Jerry replaces the cheese with a bowl of cream. Tom, hiding behind

Tom tries the "scientific" approach to mouse catching – but Jerry is ahead in this game. In Mouse Trouble, *as in most films, Tom was diligent but not terribly bright.*

the radiator, mouth watering, leaps for the cream and laps it up. Jerry releases the trap, sending Tom out the window and swinging around the tree.

"Chapter IV: A Curious Mouse is easy to catch . . . " Tom smugly strides in with a book, plops down before the mousehole, and begins to read, laughing aloud. Jerry tiptoes out and leans dangerously toward the book, but Tom turns it away and

keeps guffawing. Jerry climbs over Tom and dives into the book. Tom slams it shut. He reaches into the book and pulls out Jerry in his fist. He opens his fist and Jerry is looking at something in his own hand which he won't let Tom see. Tom strains for a peek, and Jerry pops him in the eye.

"Chapter V: A Cornered Mouse NEVER FIGHTS." Jerry, cornered and breathing hard, watches Tom's diabolical approach. Next scene: Stars flying, Tom badly bruised with a black eye, his ear twisted to one side and his whiskers frazzled. "Don't you believe it," he intones mournfully.

"Chapter VII: Be Scientific in your approach . . ." Tom, equipped with a stethoscope, listens for the mouse within the wall. Jerry, munching cheese, watches his approach. Tom finds his heartbeat and

Jerry, knowing the instrument is amplifying every sound he makes, chews on a piece of cheese and swallows, loudly. Tom snatches him up and Jerry screams into the cone.

Tom, foregoing the scientific approach, forces a shotgun into the mousehole, but the barrel bends backward, pointing at the top of his own head. Unknowingly, he fires, shearing off his hair. Next scene: He's wearing a very bad red toupee.

More determined than ever to get Jerry, he shoves a beartrap into the hole. Jerry pushes it out his back door, behind Tom, who sits back on it, leaps up and slams his head through the ceiling.

Now he tries to hit Jerry with a mallet, but Jerry comes out from behind a picture on the wall, gently removes the mallet from his paw, and hits him instead.

"Chapter IX: SLIP HIM A SURPRISE PACKAGE . . . " Tom disguises himself in a gift box tied with a bow. Jerry listens warily at the box, knocks on it, sticks hatpins into it, saws it in half, looks inside, gulps, and shows a sign, IS THERE A DOCTOR IN THE HOUSE?

Next scene: Tom, still in the toupee, with a bandage around his midsection and others dotted all over his body, is reading "Chapter XII: MICE are suckers for DAMES."

He winds up a toy girl mouse and sends it toddling past the hole, quoting Mae West, "Come up and see me some time." Jerry takes her arm and escorts her to the Cozy Arms, a false front hotel where Tom's open mouth waits behind the front door. Jerry ushers the doll in ahead of him. Out comes an assortment of springs and sprockets and Tom hiccups, "Come up and see me some time." His teeth fall out. He tears up the book and stomps on it.

Still hiccuping the Mae West line, Tom piles powder kegs, dynamite, firecrackers, and a Blockbuster bomb around the mousehole, puts more dynamite in the hole and lights it.

The cartoon ends with a tremendous bang. All that's left are Jerry, his mousehole (with no walls around it), a feather floating innocently down, and Tom hiccuping to heaven on a cloud, "Come up and see me some time."

QUIET PLEASE
1945

This cartoon has a twist. The main proponent, Spike the bulldog, is at the center of the action throughout, although all he does during most of the film is sleep. A series of hair-raising chases, a bottle of knock-out drops, and a mouse with an attitude contribute to this Oscar-winning entry.

Spike is laying in front of the fire, preparing for a nice nap. Just as he closes his eyes, he becomes the center of a chase between cat and mouse. Jerry runs over Spike, and Tom, in pursuit, hits him repeatedly with a frying pan. They scamper off and Spike naively goes back to sleep.

Moments later, gunshots are fired over Spike's head and Jerry hides behind his pillow. More shots; Jerry runs away and Tom uses Spike's head as a resting place for the rifle as he continues firing. Then he throws the rifle behind him, whacking the dog in the head. Spike buries his head under the pillow. But there are more slams and bangs as the battling duo return, this time with a hatchet with which they again manage to strike Spike.

This is the last straw. Spike grabs Tom by the chest and tells him he's driving him nuts; he's a nervous wreck (and no wonder!). "If I hear one more sound," he threatens, "I'm gonna skin ya alive. Get it?" Tom does get it, and so does Jerry, eavesdropping gleefully.

He taunts Tom with a cat figure scribbled on the wall, under which he has inscribed "Stinky."

Jerry then threatens to bang a frying pan with a wooden spoon, right near Spike's ears. Tom moves

The opening scene of Quiet Please. *Poor Spike is awakened by Tom trying to make a mousecake out of Jerry.*

away, rushes around out of sight behind Jerry, and plucks the pan and spoon away from him.

Jerry runs around the corner, pulling a lamp cord tight, tripping Tom who flies in the air, right toward a table full of martini glasses. Tom, still in midair, scoots the table out of the way and plops a sofa pillow on the floor to soften his fall.

But he immediately must contend with Jerry holding the rifle over Spike's head, preparing to pull the trigger. He puts his fingers in the barrels as Jerry fires.

While Tom is examining his throbbing fingers, Jerry is creating further havoc, trying to push a grandfather clock to the floor. He succeeds and the clock crashes down. Tom corks Spike's ears to keep the dog asleep.

As he heaves a sigh of relief, Jerry is preparing to throw light bulbs off the mantel. Tom catches them with a great display of juggling agility, but

Jerry sneaks up behind him, puts his tail in the light socket and he lights up like a Christmas tree.

But that's not enough. Jerry puts a roller skate under Tom's paw and sends the hapless cat, with light bulb cargo, crashing into Spike.

Spike starts to wake up so Tom picks him up and sings him back to sleep. Then, to avoid further confrontation, he pours an entire bottle of knock-out drops into the dog.

Jerry comes into the room banging a drum, but doesn't get a reaction. Tom pulls the drum away from him, pounds on it and on Spike, but the dog slumbers on. Tom shows Jerry the knock-out drops and the mouse gulps, then streaks away, Tom in hot pursuit again.

Now Jerry writes out his last will. He hands it to Tom, claiming he's leaving him his "sole earthly possession – ONE CUSTARD PIE." And he lets Tom have it, right in the face.

Spike gives Tom some advice. "I'm tryin' to take a nap. A little beauty sleep, see? And you're drivin' me nuts."

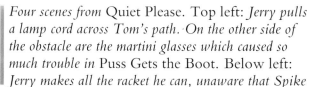

Four scenes from Quiet Please. *Top left: Jerry pulls a lamp cord across Tom's path. On the other side of the obstacle are the martini glasses which caused so much trouble in* Puss Gets the Boot. *Below left: Jerry makes all the racket he can, unaware that Spike*

has been dosed with knock-out drops. Top right: Tom chases Jerry back into Spike's territory. Below right: Tom, confused again, trades his hammer for Jerry's oversized mallet.

The chase is on again. Back into the living-room, where Spike is growling, courtesy of Jerry manipulating his sleeping mouth. Jerry barks, bites Tom in the nose and runs.

Jerry tries to revive Spike, yelling in his ear, jumping on him, stabbing him with a hatpin, but nothing works. "*Still* out cold," reads his eye when Jerry lifts the lid.

Tom comes after Jerry with a hammer, but Jerry trades him a huge mallet and Tom hands over the hammer. Jerry hits him in the foot.

Jerry puts a huge firecracker under Spike, Tom tries to pull it out, and Spike awakens. He growls at Tom, Tom shyly slides the firecracker back under the dog, and runs. Spike realizes something's wrong, and *blam!* the thing goes off. A tattered Spike rolls up his sleeve, revealing a sailor tattoo, and goes after Tom. Furniture flies through the air.

Closing scene: A bandaged Tom rocking Spike and Jerry in a cradle, while to the strains of "Rocka-bye Baby," Jerry hangs a sign that reads "Do Not Disturb."

THE CAT CONCERTO
1946

It's easy to see why this one won. Although the premise, Tom as a piano virtuoso in concert, is simple, its execution was extremely complex. Playing Liszt's Hungarian Rhapsody No. 2, Tom had to be believable doing all the fingering, and because of this, there were many gags that required special timing. Particularly deft are the many trade-offs between Tom's playing and Jerry's, neither missing a note, especially during the seamless shift from Liszt's Rhapsody to "On the Atchison, Topeka and the Santa Fe."

The cartoon opens on a grand piano spotlighted on a stage. A snooty Tom, in black tie and tails, bows formally to the audience and sits at the piano. He prepares to play, adjusting the piano stool and wiping his paws with a handkerchief. With a conceited air that can only be matched by his stuffy superiority, he begins.

Within the piano, little Jerry Mouse is sleeping on the felts. His cozy home is furnished with a lamp on an empty thread spool, two tiny chairs, and a lot of laundry, some of it monogrammed J.M.

The action of the piano jolts him around, rolling him back and forth down the felts, finally bouncing him off onto the strings. Tom plays on, unaware.

Jerry climbs up to find out what's going on and is delighted to see Tom playing. Tom is shocked to see the mouse. Jerry conducts the music with one finger. Tom uses one finger to flick him back into the piano.

Jerry stands up under a key; now he's mad. Tom plays on, pounding Jerry back under the keys. Jerry runs to and fro beneath the keys, infuriating Tom.

Tom regains control. But when he lifts his paws, the piano is still playing – Jerry is manipulating the felts from inside. Tom hits him with a tuning tool.

Undaunted, Jerry slams the keyboard cover on Tom's fingers, but the cat keeps playing (with flat fingers). Now Jerry, with a pair of scissors, tries to snip off the offending fingers. This doesn't work, so he removes a few keys and substitutes a mousetrap. Tom avoids it briefly, but at last his finger does get caught. Jerry takes over, prancing up and down on the keys.

Tom tries to catch him while still playing but Jerry dodges away. Tom climbs up onto the piano, and continuing to play with his back paws, peers inside. Not finding the mouse, he returns to position.

Suddenly the tune changes to "On the Atchison, Topeka and the Santa Fe" thanks to Jerry tap-dancing on the felts. Tom grabs him in his fist and stuffs him in the piano stool.

Jerry cranks the seat all the way up, and then, with Tom still seated on it, sends it crashing down. The virtuoso continues without missing a note.

Tom plays briskly and Jerry, once more inside the piano, gets bashed around the felts, socked in the chin, squeezed from top to bottom, and paddled from one end to the other.

Jerry breaks off two felts and, using them on the strings, takes over the music, playing faster and faster and faster. Tom, trying to maintain appearances and his fingers on the keys, can barely keep up. The piano plays on. He tries to complete the concerto, but Jerry keeps going, faster and faster.

Whiskers frazzled, coat sleeves torn, shirt front undone, Tom collapses. Jerry, pulling on a tiny tuxedo, takes a bow in the spotlight while the audience applauds.

▌ *The title frame, with its elegant neon lettering.*

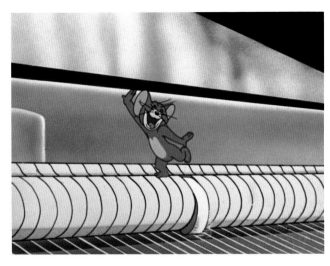

The Cat Concerto *becomes a mouse melody as* (top left) *Jerry dances "On the Atchison Topeka and the Santa Fe" on the felts. But* (top right) *Tom decides he's had enough. After this close encounter, he shoves Jerry down into the felts. Below: Jerry tries to escape, but the piano has most unusual felts.*

THE LITTLE ORPHAN
1948

Chief among the joys of this enchanting tale is the warm relationship between Jerry and little Nibbles (last seen two years earlier in *The Milky Waif*). The plucky determination with which they protect, and rescue, each other from the advancing cat, and the sheer delight with which both attack the Thanksgiving feast projects an emotional realism seldom seen in the cartoon world.

As the story opens, Jerry is sitting in his mouse-home, munching on cheese from a convenient trap and reading "Good Mousekeeping" magazine. His thimble doorbell rings and he opens the door to admit a tiny gray mouse in a cheery red cap and scarf and a diaper. Before Jerry realizes it, the little mouse is at the trap, trying to pull off the cheese.

The tyke has a note pinned to his scarf; Jerry reads it. "This is Nibbles, the little Orphan you agreed to have as your guest for dinner on Thanksgiving Day. Thank you, Bide A Wee Mouse Home. P.S. He's Always Hungry." And to demonstrate, Nibbles licks his lips.

Jerry rushes to his pantry but it's empty, not even cookies in the jar. He takes Nibbles by the hand and tiptoes to the living-room where Tom is sleeping by a bowl of cream. Jerry lifts Nibbles so he can drink from the bowl. Tom wakes up, but seeing no one, drinks the cream and goes back to sleep. Jerry holds Nibbles up so he can drink the last drop which is sliding off Tom's whisker.

Now Nibbles spots a huge feast on the dining-room table. Jerry drops down a spaghetti strand for Nibbles to use as a rope, but instead he eats his way up it. Once on the table, Nibbles, like an eating machine, toddles immediately to a pie, a celery stick, even a candle and takes several bites out of each. Jerry pulls him away, sets him down on a creampuff. The candle, breaking from Nibbles' bite, hits Jerry in the head, knocking him into the creampuff which Nibbles licks off.

The tiny mouse, spying a jello mold, uses a spoon to springboard onto it, bounces off, and tumbles toward a steaming bowl of soup. Jerry catches

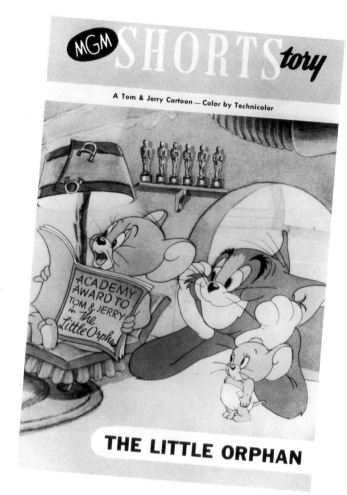

A Tom & Jerry Cartoon — Color by Technicolor

ACADEMY AWARD TO TOM & JERRY "The Little Orphan"

THE LITTLE ORPHAN

On the cover of an MGM exhibitor publication, Tom, Jerry and Nibbles bask in rave reviews of their award-winning cartoon. Said "Box Office" magazine, "It has everything a cartoon should have and a little more than some other 'greats' in the field."

him, just over the soup, with a spoon.

Now Jerry appropriates a Pilgrim hat and musket from a placecard doll, Nibbles snatches a hat too and they march across the table, stopping to fire imaginary shots at an hors d'oeuvre turkey.

Nibbles swallows a whole orange, turning into an orange-shaped mouseling. Jerry tries to extricate it by turning him upside down, but to no avail. He whacks him with a knife and the orange shoots out of Nibbles and into the sleeping Tom, giving him a very rude awakening.

Tom sneaks into the dining-room and spies mice on the table. Wearing a feather duster converted into an Indian headdress, he catches Nibbles by the tail. Jerry shoots a champagne cork at him. Yelling Indian war cries, Tom climbs on the table in pursuit of the Pilgrim mice. Nibbles grabs a fork and propelled by jello, launches an attack on Tom's rear.

Tom screeches and both mice streak away. Tom hurls the fork which catches Nibbles by his diaper. The cat takes him in his fist. Jerry climbs up a candle, carrying a spoon, and slams Tom in the face.

Left: *Jerry ponders the little whirlwind who's arrived on his doorstep, while below, they sneak up on a bowl of cream, and the cat who owns it.*

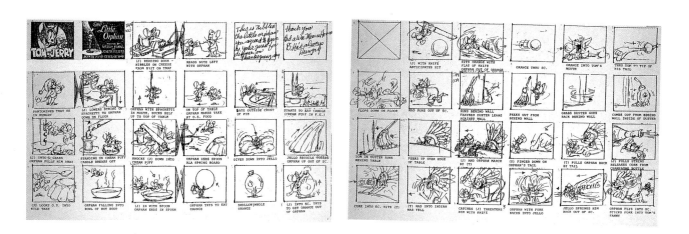

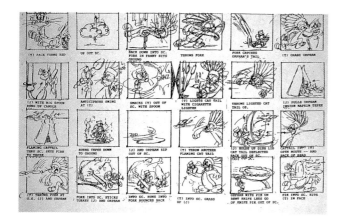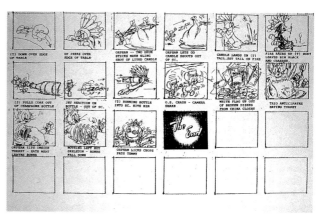

Storyboard for The Little Orphan. *The title frame with its proudly displayed Oscar appears in the actual cartoon.*

Tom's "Indian headdress" is missing most of its feathers and he's missing some fur, but truce has been declared. Here Nibbles, already airborne, gets the jump on the turkey.

Indian Tom plans an ambush. Crawling along the floor, he takes a pussy willow and sets it afire, throwing it at the mice. It burns them out of a napkin teepee and melts their butter hiding place. Another torch ricochets back to Tom and into his mouth. The mice flee, but Jerry runs into a Tom-thrown fork and is knocked flat.

Now Tom has Jerry in his clutches. Nibbles uses a knife to catapult a pie into Tom's unsuspecting face. Then he flings a flaming candle, via a turkey crossbow, which sizzles Tom. Nibbles sends a champagne bottle flying across the table. It hits Tom and hurls him across the room into a china cabinet. Tom, waving a white flag, surrenders.

Next scene: Tom, Jerry and Nibbles are saying grace at the table, loaded with steaming food. Prayers over, Tom and Jerry take up knives and forks, but Nibbles mows down the entire turkey before they have a chance to react. The cartoon closes with a very plump Nibbles licking his lips and patting his swollen tummy.

THE TWO MOUSEKETEERS
1951

Like its award-winning predecessor, *The Little Orphan*, this cartoon concerns a battle on a dining table. But instead of Indians and Pilgrims, the cat is a guard, the mice are king's musketeers, and this time, Tom's very life is on the line.

The Two Mousketeers boasts terrific displays of derring-do, with all the swashbuckling heroics of Douglas Fairbanks or Errol Flynn, and before the opening credits have dissolved from the screen, we're off with a rousing theme song, "Soldiers of Fortune," and mouseketeers Jerry and Tuffy marching down a cobbled street, brandishing their swords.

High up in a lit window, the captain of the guards is telling Tom that the table has been set for a grand banquet and he is to guard it with his very life, "especially from the king's mousketeers." If he fails, "off comes ze head." And he points out the window at a guillotine shining ominously in the moonlight. Tom, duly on guard, patrols the table.

Jerry and Tuffy enter the banquet hall through

Sensing the mouseketeer's presence, Tom looks for them on the banquet table, first one way, then the other. But he doesn't find them – yet.

74

a mouse door in the stained glass window, climb into a suit of armor and out the helmet, using their capes as parachutes to float down to the table.

Tuffy climbs up a skyscraper of swiss cheese, waving to Jerry through the holes, emerges at the top, loses his balance and falls onto a banana. Jerry swallows it whole, becoming an elongated dachshund mouse.

The mice, ever aware of the possibilities of champagne, open a bottle using a roast pig's tail as a corkscrew. The bubbly liquid shoots out, hitting Tom in the face, and collapsing them under the bottle. They hide in the roast, disguised with little caps.

Tuffy, singing "Frère Jacques" to himself, makes a ham sandwich, but Tom catches him in the act. Tuffy is quite affronted with being poked in the tush until he realizes who has done this dastardly deed. "Au secours, au secours, le pussy cat!" he yelps. Tom impales him, through his cape, on his sword.

Tuffy, poked with Tom's sword, tells him off. "Attention là! Vous pourriez faire mal a quelqu'un, Monsieur Pussy Cat!"

Jerry flies to the rescue on a curtain, stabs Tom in the tush, flings him in the air and runs onto a cake. In a wonderful display of fencing, Jerry uses a spoon to fling custard in Tom's face, plows through a dish of mashed potatoes and up onto a chicken, with the action never pausing. When Jerry can go no further, Tom catches him in his fist.

Tuffy lets loose the halberd from the suit of armor, which shears off Tom's back, revealing ruffled undershorts. Pursued by the cat, the miniature mousketeer ends up head down in a glass of champagne.

After drinking all the bubbly, Tuffy walks down the side of the glass, lifts Tom's cape, hiccups, and skewers him with his sword. "Touché, pussy cat."

But the battle isn't over. Tom grabs Tuffy but Jerry hits him with a club and the two mice dash away. Tucking Tuffy safely out of the way, Jerry swashbuckles again with Tom.

Tuffy pulls around a cannon and stuffs it full of food – pork chops, a whole chicken, tomatoes, every edible thing on the table, then lights the cannon. Explosion.

We return to the street outside the banquet room at night. Tuffy and Jerry are munching happily on sausages and cheese. "Soldier of Fortune" plays rousingly in the background. Suddenly everything stops, quiet, as a drum rolls and the guillotine slashes down.

The mouseketeers swallow hard. "Pauvre, pauvre, pussy cat," says Tuffy sadly. Then he shrugs, very gallic. "C'est la guerre." And they march off into the moonlit distance, their theme song rising to a triumphant finish.

When Tom skewers the tiny mouseketeer by his cape, Tuffy decides to take another tack. "Bonjour, Monsieur Pussy Cat." Tuffy's role as a gallic mouse was born when Hanna and Barbera heard a six-year-old girl speaking French.

JOHANN MOUSE
1952

The charm of this gem-like little film is its story-book setting. Narrated by the familiar voice of Hans Conreid, it has the look of a well-loved fairy tale. Delicately painted watercolors describe exquisitely detailed rooms, from the gold leaf on the walls to the filigree on a grand piano. The score, Strauss' lilting waltz music, performed by piano maestro Jakob Gimpel, adds to the Old World aura.

Tom and Jerry behave with continental grace, damaging throughout the cartoon only one poker and one window, seeming themselves to have been enchanted by this little story.

The cartoon opens on a book, *Johann Mouse*, and moves on to pan pages illustrated with views of Vienna in the 1800s.

"This is the story of a dancing mouse," begins Hans Conreid. "His name was Johann and he lived in Vienna in the home of Johann Strauss. Each day, as the famous musician played, little Johann couldn't resist waltzing to the beautiful music."

And we see Jerry (aka Johann) dancing in front of his mousehole with a tassel partner. At the end of the waltz, he gallantly kisses it.

"And each day, watching and waiting, was the cat." Tom dances with his back paws, while with his front ones he peers around the corner.

"Every day he would try to catch him." Johann runs into his mousehole and Tom slams into the wall. "But he would fail."

"However, this didn't discourage the cat because he knew that every day when the master played, the mouse would waltz and the cat would

In the Strauss parlor, Tom tries again and again to catch Johann to the tune of the waltz music. A studio blurb explained: "Extensive research was done on the appearance of Johann Strauss' home in Vienna and the ballroom of Austria's Imperial Country Palace – both used as scenes for the cartoon comedy."

try again." Tom slams his head again. "And again." And again slams his head into the wall. "And again." Tom slides down a bannister and crashes through the window, while little Johann cheerfully dances back into his hole.

"One day the master went away on a journey." Tom watches out the window as the carriage rolls away. "This left the cat in a serious predicament. He knew that if there were no music, the mouse wouldn't waltz."

Tom finds a book on the piano, "How To Play the Waltz in Six Easy Lessons by Johann Strauss," and picks it up.

The servants have to come to see who's playing the music, and cat and mouse respond to their applause like the troupers they are.

"Why couldn't he, the cat, learn to play?" Tom rushes, with the book, upstairs to the attic and teaches himself, lesson by lesson, note by note, and soon is playing a beautiful waltz. He closes the piano lid, wearing a devious expression.

In the salon, he begins to play and Johann, entranced, comes waltzing out of his hole. But, while

Tom is playing, he's also trying to hit Johann with a poker. The mouse runs away, but Tom returns to the piano and begins to play anew. Almost to the safety of his hole, Johann turns around, mesmerized, and begins waltzing again.

"Poor little Johann . . . he was under the spell of the beautiful music. But luckily for him, the servants wondered who was playing." Tom, meanwhile, is playing with his feet, trying to reach Johann. He grabs him. The servants applaud. He puts the mouse down and returns once again to the keyboard. Johann dances again.

"Amazing, a cat that could play and a mouse that could dance. The maid told the butcher boy. The butcher boy told the crowd in the square. Then, one of the palace guards overheard. A cat that could play and a mouse that could waltz. Good heavens! The emperor couldn't believe his ears. So they were commanded to perform at the palace at once."

The next scene: A ballroom lined with ladies and gentlemen, a grand piano in the center of its polished floor. Tom, in a suit and cravat, begins to play and Jerry, in little green tails, to dance on the piano, leaping and twirling, using Tom's paw as a partner.

"Wonderful! Sensational! And they were very happy, as long as the cat played and the mouse danced. But when the cat stopped playing . . ." Tom chases Jerry into a mousehole and smacks his head again . . . "it was the same old story."

Jerry dances into his mousehole, comes out to take a bow, and Tom turns the page. The End.

Hostilities resumed, Tom, having performed the piano fingering with his feet, succeeds in capturing Johann. As the studio publication explained, "Jerry had his waltz routine demonstrated and chartered by Dance Director Alex Romero – who performs similar choreographic services for Debbie Reynolds, Jane Powell, Janet Leigh and other glamorous MGM stars."

THE TELEVISION ERA

With seven Academy Awards under their belts, Hanna, Barbera and their staff hummed complacently along. In the greater world, storm clouds were gathering, but in their corner of the MGM lot, the only rain was the man-made kind, fifty feet from their building, where Gene Kelly was filming *Singin' in the Rain*.

The first shadows of real clouds were felt in the office of Fred Quimby, producer for not only Tom & Jerry but the entire MGM cartoon division. Since 1937 he had ridden herd on a zany cast of cartoonists of whom he understood little, having, unfortunately for a cartoon producer, no sense of humor to call upon.

Common belief on the main lot was that Quimby had won his producer's title due to long years of service as a top salesman in New York, from whence he came. Indeed, he knew nothing of animation and, as Irv Spence recalls, cartoons "were a strange thing to him."

Cast in the role of high school principal opposite the animators' boyish enthusiasms, he acted as liaison between them and the front office, usually, it seemed, turning down requests for bigger budgets, raises and special dispensations of funds.

But under his stewardship, Tom & Jerry sailed along like a flagship on a balmy sea. Not burdened with the need to deal directly with the cantankerous corporate minds in the administration arena, Hanna and Barbera were free to exercise the creativity that made Tom and Jerry the "Gold Dust Twins" of MGM.

After 18 years at the helm of the Cartoon Department, Quimby retired, and here was where the storm clouds first began to glimmer.

The Winds of Change

Quimby's retirement in no way hampered the creative flow of the Tom & Jerry cartoons, but his leaving signalled the beginning of the end of an era, the Golden Age of Hollywood, in the worlds of both live action and animation.

And the world was already beginning to change. Television, that great engulfing box with the knobs and the convex screen, was already gulping up huge chunks of the theatrical audience, allowing them to be entertained on dark evenings without ever leaving home.

Box office receipts fell, and then plummeted.

Two action sequences displaying
Jerry's lightning agility. Note the
change of expression as he goes.

Movie studios began to worry, and then to panic. New techniques were put into operation, among them CinemaScope, which widened the theater screen to provide a presumably more encompassing view of the world.

Cartoons, too, were forced to submit to the CinemaScope rage. Tom and Jerry's first such outing was *Pet Peeve*, in 1954.

Besides the change to widescreen, *Pet Peeve* was different from its predecessors in other respects. The CinemaScope process required thicker, more defined ink lines around the characters due to the fact that any imperfection would loom up on the screen. This modernized Spike, Jerry and especially Tom, smoothing out the roughness that helped make him the endearing rogue he was.

Another difference was the absence of Mammy, whose good-natured scolding and firm hand in the household had frequently given the cartoon plots their direction and pace.

Now the amply upholstered Mammy was replaced with a pale and willowy married couple. Young moderns – yuppies – of the 1950s, they were stylish, but somehow didn't have a patch on her comfortable slippers and brightly colored stockings with reinforced heels.

We know that there are only the two of them in the home because of the argument which starts off

Pet Peeve. With two acknowledged animals in the house, Tom and Spike, both happily eating their way through the refrigerator, the couple decide that food costs are too high and only one can remain as pet of the manor. Spike is the lucky pup, the husband declares, because he's *his* dog, while the wife claims that Tom is *her* cat. This springboards the story into action and utilizes the husband-wife team much as Mammy was used before.

While the tenor of Tom and Jerry's household had changed, so had that of their production staff. With Quimby's retirement, Hanna and Barbera were made producers of the series. Shouldering administrative and accounting tasks as well as carrying on their directorial work, they went on as before. But the industry-wide panic seems in some cases to have caught insidious hold.

Most of their films were still very funny, *Muscle Beach Tom*, for example, in which Tom, ever the Saturday Romeo, tries to woo a female feline sunbather. But a few, notably *Tot Watchers* (which turned out to be their last cartoon), were somehow lacking in the ebullient effervescence which characterized the series, as though its creators had already given up the ship and were merely going through the motions.

This was perhaps due to the doom which finally befell them. In 1957, MGM abruptly shut down the cartoon division, leaving Tom & Jerry once again in cartoon limbo and Hanna, Barbera and staff without a job.

Down and Outing *was Gene Deitch's second foray into the world of Tom & Jerry. Here, after the hair-raising trip to the lake, Tom's master is still quite perturbed. Notice how cat and man are wearing identical shorts. (Jerry, in the picnic basket, is too.)*

It's Greek to Me-Ow, *another Deitch episode, has Jerry living in a Doric mousehole replete with marble floors and columns. In this frame, he has just put the trash out into a Greek pillar ashcan.*

But he doesn't know that hungry Tom is searching for food in the very next ashcan. And the battle begins.

Four scenes from Chuck Jones' Rock 'n' Rodent.
Top left: Tom, in his basket bed, alarm set for the morning, prepares for sleep by reading a relaxing book.

Below left: In his mousehole in the same room, Jerry prepares for a night out.

Top right: Down in the cellar club, the bartender has set a cheese martini in front of Jerry. Jerry eats the cheese and leaves the martini for the barkeep, who gladly quaffs it.

Below right: Jerry, the band's star drummer, and his group, a radical bunch of rats.

The studio had discovered years earlier that re-releases of Tom & Jerry cartoons did as well at the box office as new ones and had instituted a policy of reissuing four cartoons made four years previously and adding them to the current releases.

Finding itself, along with every other studio in Hollywood, increasingly cash poor, MGM decided to stay with the reissues and close down the factory on the new models. And so, with no smoke signals, no warning, the Cartoon Department suddenly ceased to exist.

As Joe Barbera remembers it, "They didn't even call us. They called the accountant downstairs." Catapulted from a magical kingdom where even the waitresses in the commissary were secure enough to dump icy bowls of butter on snippy patrons, Hanna and Barbera were sent reeling from the fall.

They oversaw the finishing touches on the cartoons that had been in mid-production when the blow came, and one imagines them sleepwalking through the studio like people in shock.

"We didn't have anything to do," recalls Bill Hanna. "We saw the rest of our cartoons through, but we knew they weren't going to pick them up."

This event, terrible as it seemed at the time, was the beginning of a whole new era for Hanna, Barbera, and the world of animation.

Cartoon production at other studios was limited and no one was doing any hiring. At the eleventh hour, when their contract was at an end, Joe and Bill conceived of the idea of selling a new cartoon series to television. This was radically new thinking.

Creating Ruff and Reddy, a dog and cat team who would hopefully follow in the successful footsteps of Tom and Jerry, they sold the concept to Screen Gems, a division of Columbia Pictures. But there was a catch.

"After a lot of discussion," recalls Joe Barbera, "they decided to order five (episodes) from the storyboard I had done. We had averaged $45,000 to $65,000 (at MGM) and the most you could get from them was $3,000 for a five minute cartoon. Which meant we had to use every gimmick and schtick we knew about the business to make these things move around."

Thus, limited animation was born.

Tom & Jerry had alway been fully animated. When they gave each other a glare or a happy glance, they used not only facial expression but body language, creating the image of living beings.

In limited animation, there is neither time nor money to expend on such niceties. As Lefty Callahan explains, "You can hold the body (meaning that the body remains static) and put the arms on separate levels (separate cels), the mouth, the eyes, everything. You can blink the eyes and not move anything else. If the body is held and you reach out for something, only the arms move."

At the newly formed Hanna-Barbera Productions, making cartoons with this technique was like having a tiger by the tail. You just grabbed hold,

The Year of the Mouse, *another Chuck Jones outing. Here, Tom, believing he's hit himself with a flyswatter in his sleep (it was actually Jerry who did it), fluffs up his pillow for another try at catnapping. In another scene from the same cartoon, Tom is having a most unrestful day. Jerry and his mouse cohort have led him to think he's shot at himself. Then he finds himself tugging on a rope slung around his neck and attached to a light fixture on the ceiling. This publicity shot shows what happens next. (Jerry was added later, along with the logo.)*

Stills from the Hanna-Barbera Productions television version of Tom & Jerry. Though they looked the same as in MGM days, they could have been anybody. The joyous animosity was gone. In other departures from the "old" Tom and Jerry, the two always walked upright, Jerry always appeared in a little red bow tie, and rather than holding the simple jobs of cat and mouse, they worked at other employments and endured various on the job adventures. The series didn't work, but it was a valiant try.

Jerry is an avid science fiction buff in Invasion of the Mouse Snatchers, *a Filmation cartoon. Here, after seeing a monster (Tom in disguise) emerge from a flying saucer, he hurriedly consults his comic books for identification of the creature.*

The very next frame, showing minute changes in expression and posture. Notice the delightful attention to details – the space station hanging from the ceiling, space gun slung over the bedpost, the science fiction magazines strewn around the room.

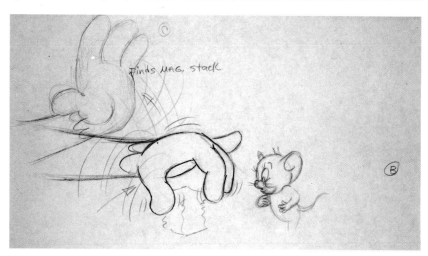

finds MAG. stack

Tom searches through Jerry's comic collection for a picture of a suitably scary space monster. This rough sketch shows how his hand will reach into Jerry's bedroom, rifling through the books with diabolical glee.

92

and tried desperately to keep pace.

At MGM, Bill Hanna recalls, "We made six or eight of those little six minute cartoons a year. If we did a hundred feet a week, we thought we were doing pretty good. When we started into television, we would do as much as a hundred feet an hour."

The pace of life had changed entirely, but not for the worse. From Ruff and Reddy, Hanna-Barbera went on to create dozens of successful characters, Huckleberry Hound, Yogi Bear, The Flintstones, and The Jetsons, to name only a few. They purchased a six acre parcel, mysteriously called "The Monkey Farm," in Hollywood and built the studio they still occupy today.

But Tom & Jerry were still in cartoon limbo.

Then, with the dawn of the 1960s came a new lease on life. MGM had decided that its "Gold Dust Twins" might still be viable properties after all, and Gene Deitch was signed to produce 13 new shorts.

Below: *In the opening scene of Invasion of the Mouse Snatchers, Tom is at it again. In moments, he, rather than Jerry, will be knocking plates off the mantel.*

Bottom: *The "space monster," looking for the perfect cherry, makes Jerry pick all the fruit off the backyard tree.*

On Foreign Assignment

Deitch's credits included a stint as artistic director of Terrytoons, where he created the critically acclaimed "Tom Terrific," a sparsely but imaginatively drawn series for the "Captain Kangaroo" children's TV program, and "Munro," a theatrical short for which he won an Oscar.

He had recently moved self and studio to Prague and his Czechoslovakian animators had only half a dozen Tom & Jerry cartoons to use in familiarizing themselves with their new characters.

In contrast to Hanna, Barbera, Irv Spence, Ken Muse and the other animators at MGM, who collectively *were* Tom & Jerry, the Eastern European team never stood a chance of continuing the old magic.

Although they managed to retain the basic look of the characters – if you bumped into them on the street you'd probably recognize them – they didn't act like Tom and Jerry. Jerry, whose winsome looks contributed a great deal to his charm, was glossed over, somehow giving the impression of being viewed through the wrong end of a telescope, and Tom had lost the irrepressibly devious quality that gave personality to his movements, becoming instead just another character dashing across the screen.

Gone were the fine details that polished their performance, throwaway moments like Tom licking his lips over a bowl of cream, or a mouse, or Jerry bravely squaring his shoulders to protect tiny Tuffy.

Music and sound effects, that had been so important to the "old" Tom & Jerrys, actually detracted from the action, leaving the cat and mouse to fend for themselves.

The climax of Invasion of the Mouse Snatchers: *in desperation Jerry radios a distress signal to all the rodents in the city, who band together to create a supermouse, shown here grasping Tom.*

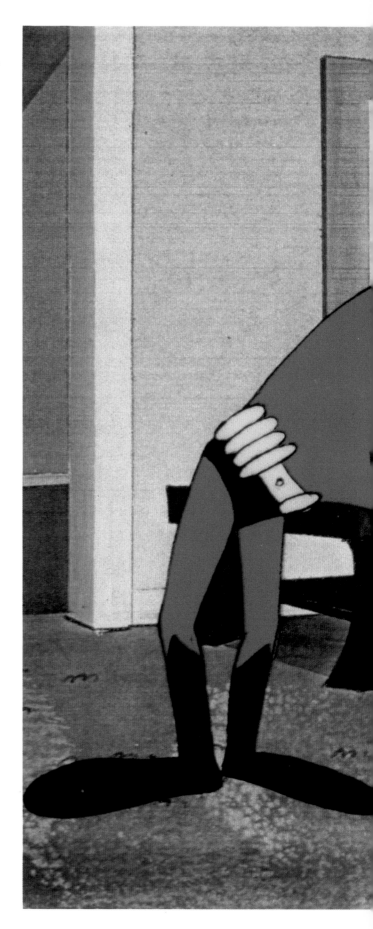

Publicity stills for Filmation's version of Tom & Jerry. Reverting back from the Hanna-Barbera TV version, they were once again in the home with food fights in the kitchen and chases through the living-room, though the requisite bashes and bangs were still banned by children's programming guidelines.

These Filmation scenes are reminiscent of the early Hanna and Barbera/MGM The Night Before Christmas, *except that here it is Tom and not Jerry who's out in the cold.*

Despite all this, there were likable elements. In *Down and Outing*, which has much of the action set in a moving automobile, Jerry pushes on the accelerator, leaving the driver (and everyone else on the road) a nervous wreck and Tom the object of blame. In *Tall in the Trap*, set in a Western frontier town, a row of saloons all bear names like the "Rigor Mortis . . . Come In and Get Stiff," and the "Six Gun . . . Come In and Get Loaded."

The overall cartoons, however, fell short of the originals on which they were based, and Deitch's contract was not extended beyond the first 13.

Instead, in 1962, MGM packaged together 18 of the Hanna and Barbera era shorts, labeled them the "Tom & Jerry Festival of Fun," and sent them round the theaters as a feature in their own right. This proved to the studio that audiences still loved the cat and mouse, and it decided to try again.

Back in the U.S.A.

When Warner Brothers closed its cartoon doors in 1963, MGM jumped in and offered Chuck Jones the opportunity to animate new Tom & Jerrys for theatrical release. Jones was a veteran, and very talented, animator, having been intrinsic to the development of Warner's stars Bugs Bunny, Daffy Duck and their brethren.

He set to work, making his first task a remodel of the famous duo. Tom was given Boris Karloff eyebrows that enhanced his diabolical demeanor, and in many poses bears a strong resemblance to Bugs himself, with a tail and cropped ears. Jerry received larger, more winsome eyes, larger ears, and a sweeter expression.

The Tom & Jerry logo received a facelift, too, with the old title frame replaced by a spiffier 1960s one and new, tinkly music signature. Even Leo, the MGM lion, who had appeared at the beginning of every cartoon since the studio's beginning, was replaced in mid-roar by Tom meowing and hissing into the camera.

But these are not the only differences between the vintage Tom & Jerrys and Jones'. Graphically stylish and brightly colored, the latter veered

Notice the difference between these Filmation television era cels and the theatrical releases. Tom has been streamlined just a bit more – enough to facilitate limited animation's need for rapid reproduction, and his movements are more static; although entertaining, they don't leap off the cel with action and life.

toward poses and personality. Much like Bugs' plots, they often started out strong and got side-tracked by other ideas. Although this style fit other Jones formats, Tom & Jerry were not the same without a solid story behind them.

The opening credits were highly imaginative, with the titles, often clever wordplays, worked into the context of the cartoon itself.

This is a fun little film in which Jerry, a drummer at a hep joint in the basement, totally unnerves a sleep-starved Tom. In this cartoon, elements of the "old" Tom & Jerry are still evident. The ample detail is delightful, and the atmosphere of a smoky bar is rounded out by the other rodents in the band.

The Year of the Mouse was more in the new tradition of Chuck Jones, who had a different slant on the cat and mouse. Jerry and a mouse cohort attempt to gaslight Tom by placing various lethal weapons in his hands while he's asleep. In a sly bit of role reversal, Tom, finally figuring out the plot at the tale's end, corks Jerry in a bottle from which there is no non-lethal exit.

After 34 such cartoons, MGM in 1967 stopped production. Believing there was no future in theatrical cartoons, the studio chose not to renew its contract with Jones, and Tom and Jerry were again relegated to the dusty archives of the studio library.

Two model sheets for Tom and Jerry Kids. *Notice Tom's child-like pout, very different from his adult scowl, and Jerry's more child-like strut.*

Teaming Up for Television

Eight years later, in 1975, Hanna and Barbera, the original Tom & Jerry men, came up with the notion of casting their old friends in a new series for Saturday morning television.

It was a difficult sell. Network executives, while laughing heartily during screenings of the old cartoons, feared that they were too violent and would be panned by parents' groups. As a compromise, Hanna-Barbera agreed to revamp the characters (again!).

Tom and Jerry had always been backstage buddies, and in their latest incarnation they were pals on-screen as well, spending their cartoon hour in friendly competition, solving mysteries and helping others.

The new series, officially called "The New Tom & Jerry/ Grape Ape Show" (sharing the hour were stories featuring a giant purple gorilla), often placed them in a variety of situations other than their home.

Various episodes had them as bullfighters, police officers, stunt "men" and a mad scientist's assistants.

In *Stay Awake or Else . . .*, they are circus roustabouts, with the ringmaster threatening to fire an exhausted Tom if he falls asleep on the job. Jerry tries his best to make the somnolent cat appear awake, including putting him on roller skates with a broom in his paw.

The Kids title frame. One must wait for the closing credits to note that the story editor is Neal Barbera, Joe's son, and the director is Ray Patterson, one of the original MGM era animators, still with Tom & Jerry after all these years. Below: Two publicity stills from the program.

• NOTE - TREES ARE LIGHT ON DARK.
• USE WARM COLOR AGAINST COOL COLORS.

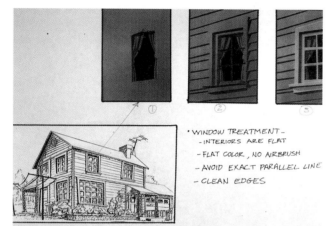

• WINDOW TREATMENT -
  - INTERIORS ARE FLAT
  - FLAT COLOR, NO AIRBRUSH
  - AVOID EXACT PARALLEL LINE
  - CLEAN EDGES

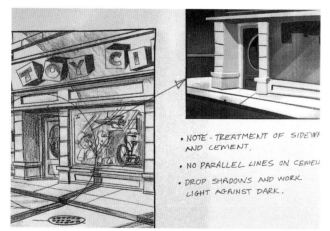

• NOTE - TREATMENT OF SIDEWA AND CEMENT.
• NO PARALLEL LINES ON CEMEN
• DROP SHADOWS AND WORK LIGHT AGAINST DARK.

"How-to" backgrounds for the Kids. *Because the ink and paint work is farmed out to other countries, instructions must be very explicit. "If you don't have a strong style," says Al Gmuer, Hanna-Barbera studio based background artist, "it flattens and loses all the flavor."*

No Bones About It has them searching for a valuable dinosaur bone missing from the museum where they work. In a plot which harks back to *Bringing Up Baby*, a gem of a screwball comedy with Cary Grant and Katharine Hepburn circa 1938, they go after a dog who apparently has stolen the bone, using every means possible to retrieve it.

The stories were both inventive (termites as a motorcycle gang with rotary sawblades for wheels) and fondly reminiscent of the Golden Age of Comedy (one episode, a la Laurel and Hardy, found them trying to move a heavy safe up a steep hill, with calamitous results), but neither the children at whom the show was aimed nor their parents really warmed to the battling buddies as non-violent pals. Somehow, the truth that had always been so readable under the surface, that Tom and Jerry never really wanted to hurt each other – that it was the excitement of the chase that mattered – came through loud and clear here as well, in that it was missing.

And although the program was rerun in various co-starring formats (with a dog detective and his assistant), it never quite took hold and eventually was dropped.

In 1980, MGM Television leased Tom & Jerry to the CBS television network for a series called "The Tom & Jerry Comedy Show." This was a new batch of cartoons produced for TV by Filmation, a studio specializing in limited animation for the tube. But again, the sparkle was missing, and the series faded after a single season.

MGM, the Golden Age studio with the heavenly host of stars, was acquired by Turner Broadcasting Systems in 1986, and along with its priceless library of movie magic, turned over all rights to Tom & Jerry. TBS fully realized the treasure that had been trothed to them, and immediately began television airings of theatrical era Tom & Jerry cartoons.

In 1989, Hanna-Barbera started production on a new Saturday morning television series, "Tom & Jerry Kids," featuring the cat and mouse as children. Plot lines put them in various locations, such as every child's dream setting – the toy store.

Animating the "Kids" presented new problems for the animators to solve. Because they are younger, they must move differently than their "adult" counterparts. Shorter legs, youthful exuberance and a bit of wobbling on the pins contribute to the childish air.

Hanna and Barbera are now hard at work on the next grouping. The series seems to be working, and that's what its creators are striving for.

"Every time we previewed a cartoon," Joe Barbera says, recalling their MGM days, "people didn't know what they were going to get. And all of a sudden, it would come on the screen – Tom & Jerry – and the yell that went up would make you feel good for 20 years. That's what I hope we do again with these (younger) characters."

Carefully thought out and delightfully executed backgrounds for the Kids *series. "It's all a matter of staging," says Mr Gmuer. "A monster show you don't want bright backgrounds, you want gloomy backgrounds . . . It's a challenge; every one of them's different. That's what keeps it fresh for us."*

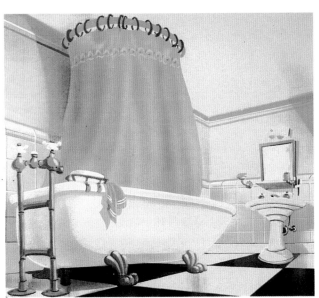

TOM and JERRY TIE-INS

Tom and Jerry's success at the box office spawned a myriad of tie-in materials, much as Shirley Temple's curls promoted paper doll sales and Vivien Leigh's performance in *Gone With the Wind* prompted merchandisers to introduce Scarlett O'Hara perfumes.

And while no one thought to market eau de fromage or essence of cream, there have been a host of products stamped with the Tom & Jerry style through the years.

Beginning in their Hanna Barbera heyday at MGM, one could purchase any number of items to both warm the body and adorn it: silk mufflers, scarves and handkerchiefs, all decorated with a Tom & Jerry motif; brooches, barrettes, charm bracelets, and earrings; sweatshirts, suspenders and slipper socks.

For entertainment when Tom and Jerry weren't playing at the movies, there were board games, balloons, bicycle horns, puppets, and all manner of books: paint books, storybooks, flip books, and of course, comic books.

These novelties, aimed mainly at children, would tide the tried and true Tom & Jerry fan

Tom & Jerry at the bookstore. Notice the MGM blurb, aimed at "alert exhibitors."

TOM & JERRY CERAMICS

decorative as well as useful . . . a complete line including figurines, book-ends, flower pots, doorstops, cigarette containers, etc.

TOM & JERRY PUPPETS AND BICYCLE HORNS
(DROOPY AND BARNEY BEAR, TOO . . .)

through the long hours until a trip to the movies could be arranged from raided piggybanks or suitably sweet-talked parents.

This would purchase entrance to a Saturday morning Cartoon Club where, in a heaven redolent of popcorn and jujubes, a kid could sit through as many as ten cartoons at a time.

Some theaters, like the Gem, in St Johns, Missouri, discovered that a "Cartoon Picnic" featuring Tom & Jerry in an all-cartoon evening brought capacity crowds, with grown-ups far outnumbering the children, and a parade of hundreds of patrons waiting outside in the chill spring evening for the show to begin.

Movie exhibitors found Tom & Jerry a wide-open market. According to an MGM publicity blurb, "Each Tom & Jerry release plays approximately 22,000 U.S. theatre bookings. Considering there are only 15,000 theaters operating in the country, this means repeat bookings at many movie houses."

When the Dark Ages hit the studios and MGM was no longer making Tom & Jerrys, legions of fans still followed them on television where careful channel searching would reward the seeker with vintage cartoons still showing, and still funny.

Today the dueling duo are shown daily in almost 50 countries all over the world, including such seemingly out-of-the-way locales as Algeria, Iceland, and Bolivia.

For those who can't find Tom & Jerry on television – or can't wait – videotapes of all-time favorites are packaged for sale or rent.

The die-hard fan can even have a Tom & Jerry fancy dress party, with costumes for adults and children. Invitations, balloons, paper plates, plastic cutlery, hats and horns . . . everything one could want for a bash is available in a Tom & Jerry theme.

TOM & JERRY T-SHIRTS and SWEAT SHIRTS
SUITABLE FOR BOYS OR GIRLS —

A wonderful profusion of Tom & Jerry tie-in merchandise. These photographs are from an MGM booklet designed to educate exhibitors on licensing possibilities.

Millions follow the antics of TOM & JERRY daily in the TOM & JERRY COMIC STRIP ... syndicated by the mighty AP ...

The ever-popular TOM AND JERRY Comic Book—a new one every month—sold on newsstands across the country. Everyone's favorite!

A Christmas greeting from Tom and Jerry to their studio colleagues.

A poster heralding Tom & Jerry's success in the television market.

The Tom & Jerry Household

Once again, as in the golden days of MGM, a rich panoply of tie-in merchandise is available. You can perk up your home team pep rallies with Tom, Jerry and Tuffy on college logo t-shirts and sweatshirts. Or sleep in a complete Tom & Jerry bedroom, starting with the headboard, duvet cover, pillow slips, and pillow pals, finishing off with wall coverings, borders and curtains, while giant four-foot plush Tom & Jerry characters stand watch.

Then move on to the bath, with battery operated toothbrushes, toothpaste, bubble bath and shampoo, even a Tom & Jerry soapmaker.

There are pages of other tie-in merchandise for everyone from the infant to the well-dressed executive (Tom & Jerry boxer shorts, briefcase and 24k gold-plated wristwatch). The junior executive can be equipped with a plastic wristwatch and a Tom & Jerry lunch box. And for mum, at the shops, the Tom & Jerry plastic credit card.

From kitchens full of Tom & Jerry coffee mugs, cookie jars, cake mix and teapots to camp sites with Tom & Jerry sleeping bags, canteen, flashlight and binoculars; from satin jackets to nighties and pajamas, body tattoos to boxed stationery, the Tom & Jerry fan will never want for something different.

Tom & Jerry were hot copy, discussed in many magazine articles. They appeared frequently on the cover of "Rexall Magazine," a publication of the national drugstore chain.

APRIL · 1949

M-G-M's Tom and Jerry and their version of April Showers.

SEASON'S GREETINGS

Tom and Jerry

This cheery message was part of an MGM Records puff piece which explained that the cat and mouse "have become as much a part of the motion picture scene as the corner of Hollywood and Vine and as much a part of the kiddie corner in the record department as Rudolph, that famous red-nose reindeer."

"MGM ShortStory," shown on the facing page, was a fold-out booklet sent to exhibitors, priming them on cartoon shorts the studio believed worthy of extra attention, in this case the justifiably exalted *The Cat Concerto*. Notice the oval framed "Family Portrait" offered free to exhibitors for lobby or window displays. An inside page shows Fred Quimby accepting the award, while the fold-out features various posters and ad mats available to exhibitors, plus articles which could be run in local newspapers. A "Box Office Angles" column detailed methods for bringing in patrons, such as giving free tickets to piano teachers and their more proficient students.

Tom & Jerry Top Cartoon Stars!

In the few short years since Tom & Jerry first came off the drawing boards of MGM's Cartoon Department, the two pen-and-ink personalities have become ranking Cartoon stars. In the past seven years, they have won the Academy Award for "the best Cartoon of the year" — five times — a record unmatched by any other Cartoon stars or series. This year's winner "The Cat Concerto" may now be seen at the....Theatre.

In "The Cat Concerto," the famous filmic feud between Tom & Jerry takes a symphonic turn as the cat goes highbrow to don white tie and tails and tackle Liszt's Second Hungarian Rhapsody at the piano. Jerry Mouse, never one to miss an opportunity, finds this a chance to perform a bit of mischief. A melange of melody, mirth and mayhem follows to make "The Cat Concerto" an unique and memorable bit of musical tomfoolery.

Fred C. ...

Tom Cat takes the situation in hand when Jerry Mouse interrupts his piano playing in "The Cat Concerto," MGM's Academy Award winning Tom & Jerry Cartoon now at the   Theatre.

Maestro Tom Cat does a bit of tricky keyboard work as Jerry Mouse looks on disapprovingly. Scene from MGM's Academy Award winning Tom & Jerry Cartoon "The Cat Concerto" now at the   Theatre.

QUIMBY COLLECTS "OSCARS"

Winning Academy Awards has become a habit with MGM Cartoon Producer Fred C. Quimby, whose latest production, "The Cat Concerto" has ... won the Oscar as "the best Cartoon ..." This makes the fifth ...

1943 by "Yankee Doodle Mouse"; "Mouse Trouble" in 1944 and "Quiet Please," last year's winner.

"The Cat Concerto" presents Tom & Jerry in a musical setting — Tom as a concert pianist playing Liszt's Second Hungarian Rhapsody — and ... the role of a heckler, a ... and hi-

FRED C. QUIMBY

THE CAT CONCERTO
AN M-G-M TOM & JERRY CARTOON IN TECHNICOLOR

To the names of Joseffy, De Pachmann, Rubenstein, Schnabel and other immortal pianists, must now be added that of a new impressario — Maestro Tom Cat, concert pianist extraordinaire. ... now gives an exhibition of his virtuosity in the new MGM Tom & Jerry Cartoon, "The Cat Concerto," winner of the 1946 Academy Award as "the best cartoon of the year." It is a performance that has to be seen and heard to be believed.

Tom makes his appearance before what he hopes audience and ... gins what he hopes will be a brilliant rendition of the Liszt Second Hungarian Rhapsody. Resplendently dressed in white tie and tails, he ...

... a picture of classical dignity, and with a grandiloquent bow he begins to play. But what Mr. Liszt didn't reckon with when he composed his immortal Rhapsody was the presence of a mischievous Jerry Mouse inside the keyboard of the piano. To Jerry's anti-symphonic ear, music is nothing more than a lot of noise and he registers his disapproval by trying to break up the concert.

In the ensuing riot of music and mayhem, no piano ever took more punishment — and no pianist ever was so harassed. Chords turn into discords; arpeggios, trills and cadenzas become embroiled in a cascade of flying piano keys and hammers as ...

Jerry goes to work to systematically plague the pianist. Tom responds with his usual alacrity. Since Jerry can keep thinking up more ways to annoy his perennial foe than could be imagined, the tics of the feuding duo keep things humming at a hilarious pace until the number has come to a finish that has all but exhausted the palpitating pianist. In the end, it is a triumphant Jerry Mouse who takes the bows and receives the overwhelming ovation of the audience.

Fred Quimby produced "The Cat Concerto," which was co-directed by William Hanna and Joseph Barbera.

HERE ARE YOUR SELLING AIDS FOR "THE CAT CONCERTO"

... number in their ... Award winning MGM Technicolor Cartoon "The Cat Concerto" now at the .... Theatre.

"The Cat Concerto" starts calmly enough as Tom Cat sits down at the concert grand and begins to play, but his benign mood soon changes ...

... Maestro Tom Cat, concert pianist ... proceeds. The results of this musical mixup provide hilarious screen fare.

Tom's efforts to complete his concert finally succeed, but not until Jerry has made a shambles of the entire affair, and it is an exhausted Tom who sits panting at the piano when the music is finished.

Fred C. Quimby produced "The Cat Concerto" which was co-directed by William Hanna and Joseph Barbera.

AD MATS
Available GRATIS at National Screen Service Branches

... ject a secret ...

Cut-out figures of ... Tom & Jerry always make eye-stopping lobby, theatre front and window displays. Use them generously.

"The Cat Concerto" is a natural for tie-ups with music and piano stores. Provide them with an assortment of stills for a display that is bound to get attention.

Circularize your local piano teachers, all of whom will be especially interested in this subject. Perhaps arrangements can be made for them to bring their pupils in groups at special rates. A small quantity of guest tickets can be made available to several teachers for presentation to those pupils who show the most proficiency in their piano lessons.

Run a TOM & JERRY memory contest, offering guest tickets as prizes for the most complete list of past Tom & Jerry Cartoon titles sent in. This could be adapted for either newspaper or radio use.

Arrange a special screening of "The Cat Concerto" for local music critics. If there is a concert pianist in your locality, invite this artist to your preview. His or her reaction to "The Cat Concerto's" humorous treatment of a classical piece of music should provide interesting publicity material.

HERE ARE YOUR SELLING AIDS FOR "THE CAT CONCERTO"

All this comes in the wake of worldwide celebration of the cat and mouse team's Golden Anniversary. From Paris to Bangkok, the Louvre Museum to the Luna Park amusement center in Japan, Tom & Jerry's 50 years in show business have been honored everywhere.

In the United Kingdom, the Marks & Spencer chain of 380 stores put on a Tom & Jerry party for children with leukemia – a raving success for all concerned.

Also in the U.K., the Berni Restaurant Group used Tom & Jerry to spice up their food menu with games and puzzles; and in the U.S., McDonald's beefed up their hamburger sales with the Happy Meal Band Program. And not to leave the family pet out of the picture, Pedigree Foods used Tom & Jerry in a promotional campaign for Kit-e-Kat cat food.

Tom & Jerry had their own television special and have received the honor of being the first parade balloon to incorporate two characters as a single piece (because, of course, they are an inseparable team). The 50-foot tall balloon made its maiden voyage, riding high over the Macy's Thanksgiving Day Parade in New York City.

Not everyone can own a five-story balloon, but lots of people collect Tom & Jerry animation cels. These are hard to come by, and the avid collector must be as diligent, and as lucky, as a seeker of pirates' treasure trove.

When Hanna and Barbera left MGM, they left

Radical dudes Tom and Jerry and their vintage Woody, surfing on Aladdin's lunch kit.

behind all their cels and sketches. Years later, MGM, in a vast housecleaning enterprise, threw out all of these treasures, not realizing their value. Some were rescued on the spot by studio employees who had the foresight and the perspicacity to paw through the trash to retrieve them. Others mysteriously found their way into obscure closets and drawers and every so often surface at garage sales and flea markets. Occasionally, Hanna and Barbera receive one of these cels in the mail at their Hollywood studio, with a request from the proud new owner to have it autographed by Tom and Jerry.

A good quality cel, done in the Chuck Jones era, can bring from $450.00 to $650.00, according to Elvena Green of the One-of-a-Kind Cartoon Art Gallery in Decatur, Georgia. A cel from the Hanna-Barbera MGM heyday, if found, would bring much more.

Many Tom & Jerry lovers find it unnecessary to collect anything tangible at all. Monica Seles, a 15-year-old Yugoslavian, is a tennis pro who took lessons from the cat and mouse. "I used to pretend I was the cat chasing the tennis ball which was Jerry," Monica said in an article in the *Daily Mail*.

Like Monica, millions of people all over the world have taken Tom & Jerry into their hearts. And as their half century of entertaining gathers speed and rolls into a century, millions more will be charmed, enchanted and delighted.

Everything for the party, courtesy of Amscan of New York.

Marks & Spencer boxer shorts feature Tom & Jerry as ski bunnies or as tropical native and explorer.

Tom, Jerry, Tuffy and, on the facing page, Spike and Tyke, model their new look for the '90s. Spiffed up by Turner Entertainment in "rad" shirts, jeans and running shoes, they are all set to help advertisers show off their product lines.

Tom & Jerry's 50th birthday party at Marks & Spencer was a thrill for all concerned.

Jerry, Jerry, Quite Contrary (1966)

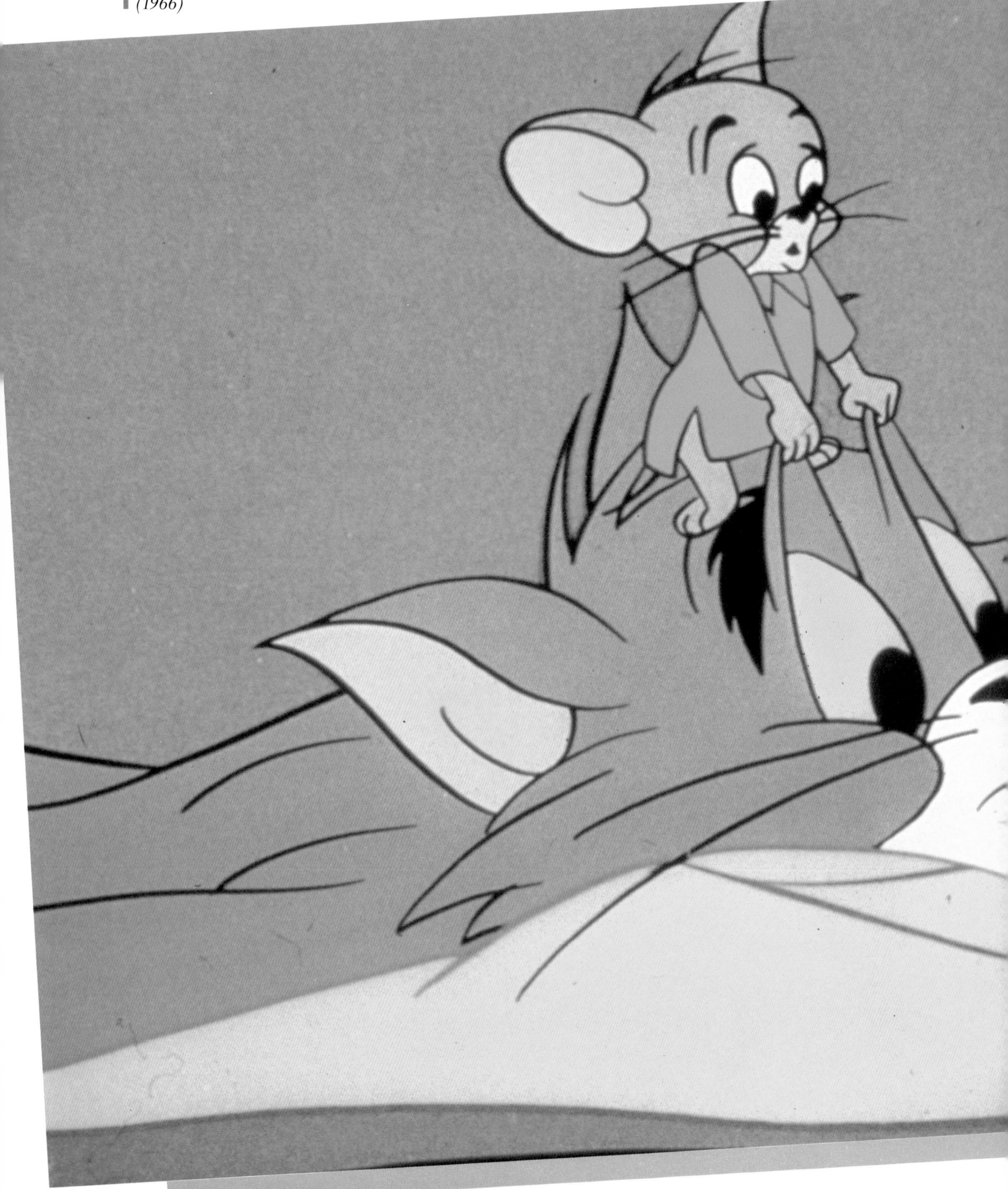

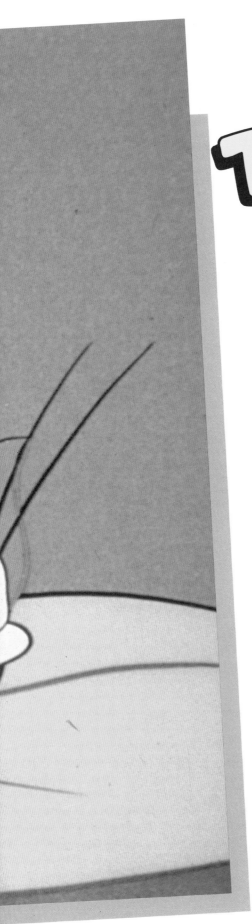

TOM and JERRY TATTLER

Remember Your Favorite Tom & Jerry Cartoons?

When MGM decided to lease their goldmine of Tom & Jerry cartoons to television, they developed a list of capsule descriptions to show potential licensees the crackerjack joys in store.

Based on the studio's actual list, the following capsules give the reader an insight into what was happening in the years the cartoons were made, the mindset of the creators, and the changes that took place in layouts, characters and storylines through the years.

Influenced by subjects ranging from world war (*The Yankee Doodle Mouse*) to the suburban barbecue craze of the 1950s (*Barbecue Brawl*) to the cold war (*The Mouse From H.U.N.G.E.R.*), Tom & Jerry's creators, consciously or not, brought these themes to the cartoon screen. Whether it was that modern new invention, the dishwasher, (the impetus for *Push-button Kitty*) or the movie mania for swashbuckling heroics (*The Two Mouseketeers*), a story idea was set into motion and brought to brilliant life.

The stories and characters that worked were retained. Tuffy, the beloved baby mouse, and

Quacker, the duckling with the stubborn streak, were featured over and over, along with Spike and his puppy son Tyke, and irascible Meathead and his cat pals. Circus animals were a popular theme, as was the replacement of Tom by a rival, and, of course, the uncertain path of true love.

Reading between the lines, one can see how these ideas popped up again and again, not only from cartoon to cartoon but from one director to another. Changes in not only stories and characters but pacing and locale hinted of changes in the world beyond the movie screen.

The original MGM list was in alphabetical order; ours is given by year. A star appears after the title of each cartoon which received an Academy Award nomination. A quick reference alphabetical listing appears in an appendix at the end of the book for added convenience.

Ready, then? Grab hold of your popcorn and let's go!

THE HANNA–BARBERA YEARS

PUSS GETS THE BOOT★
Running Time 9.15 min. *Release Date* 10 Feb 1940

In the cartoon that started it all, Mammy Two Shoes warns Tom (Jasper here), "Break one more thing and you is goin' out." Jerry (still a nameless little rodent), deciding to help his archnemesis out the door, goes for broke, tossing cocktail glasses and dishes with glee, while hapless Tom does his best at juggling. At film's end, Jasper is indeed given the boot, while Jerry struts into a mousehole adorned with the sign, "Home Sweet Home."

THE MIDNIGHT SNACK
Running Time 8.15 min. *Release Date* 19 July 1941

Back again by public demand, their second outing finds Tom and Jerry in a battle over refrigerator rights. After various skirmishes, Jerry is trapped in the icebox and discovered by Mammy. With a bit of clever maneuvering and a well-placed fork, however, mouse lands cat in the freezer, from whence he is once more given the boot.

THE NIGHT BEFORE CHRISTMAS★
Running Time 8.47 min. *Release Date* 6 Dec 1941

In this yuletide confection, Christmas Eve finds Jerry running merrily around the tree, jumping from the ornaments to a plush lion to – surprise! – Tom. After an escape trip on a toy train and an escapade with a sprig of mistletoe, he eludes Tom by clambering through the mail slot and out into the snow. But Tom won't let him back in. A distant carol softens the cat's heart, however, and he retrieves him from the cold.

FRAIDY CAT
Running Time 8.11 min. *Release Date* 17 Jan 1942

A scary radio show frightens Tom, and Jerry has a ball scaring him all the more by making a ghost from a vacuum cleaner and a nightshirt. In a lovely piece of animation, the vacuum almost sucks up Tom's nine lives. But the last laugh is on Jerry, who having fallen into a tin of flour and catching sight of his reflection, manages to scare himself as well.

A publicity still for Fraidy Cat, *in which Tom nearly loses all nine lives at once.*

Right at the outset of Dog Trouble, *Jerry traps Tom's tail. This is another publicity shot in which Jerry was added.*

DOG TROUBLE
Running Time 7.57 min. Release Date 18 Apr 1942

While Tom is chasing Jerry around the house, he runs right into a sleeping Spike, who dashes after both cat and mouse. In a joint effort with Tom to rid the house of the dog pest, Jerry winds a web of yarn around the living-room, snaring Spike and pulling over all the furnishings. Mammy finds the trapped dog and scolds him for "wreckin' up the house" as cat and mouse resume the chase. This cartoon has two distinguishing features: the debut of Spike the bulldog, and the first (but not the last!) time Tom and Jerry team up against a common enemy.

PUSS 'N' TOOTS
Running Time 7.48 min. Release Date 30 May 1942

When Mammy babysits a pretty kitten, Tom goes head over heels and offers her in turn, a goldfish, a canary, and a mouse, performing an impressive variety of parlor tricks with Jerry as the magic coin. But the tables turn when he chases Jerry onto the phonograph and becomes caught in the automatic record changer, to the hubba hubba tune of "Hold That Tiger."

THE BOWLING-ALLEY CAT
Running Time 8.00 min. Release Date 18 July 1942

Adventures in the fast lanes, as Tom chases Jerry through a bowling alley. Strikes, spares, and battles of wits ensue, until finally Jerry ties Tom's tail around the ball, and a very surprised cat goes down the alley and through the back wall. Score a strike for Jerry.

FINE FEATHERED FRIEND
Running Time 7.43 min. Release Date 10 Oct 1942

That fiendish feline Tom tries to catch Jerry·in the barnyard, but all the chicks and ducks band together to protect the little mouse, especially a mama hen. At tale's end, Jerry falls asleep under her wing.

SUFFERIN' CATS
Running Time 7.50 min. Release Date 16 Jan 1943

When Jerry is besieged by both Tom and an alley cat (Meathead, in his first screen role) who has been raised on sardine cans and old shoes, the sly mouse cleverly angles the two pursuers into one another. While they feverishly fight, Jerry escapes.

THE LONESOME MOUSE
Running Time 8.07 min. Release Date 22 May 1943

When Tom is ejected from the house yet again, Jerry thinks it's his lucky day. He swims a·lap in Tom's saucer of cream, paints a Hitler mustache on his picture, and then tears up his basket. But these antics pale beside the thrill of the chase, and Jerry, with the unwitting Mammy's assistance, gets Tom back inside where he belongs.

THE YANKEE DOODLE MOUSE
Running Time 7.23 min. Release Date 26 June 1943

In this utterly charming tribute to America's fighting men, the beleaguered Jerry, using makeshift props from the basement, builds a cat raid shelter, posts signs showing the way to safety in the event of a cat attack, drives a cheese-grater jeep, drops light bulb bombs, and issues war communiques. Thoroughly defeating enemy Tom, Jerry's final communique reads, "Send More Cats." Quite fittingly, the cartoon captured the year's Oscar.

BABY PUSS
Running Time 7.51 min. Release Date 25 Dec 1943

Forced to play baby for a little girl, Tom spots snickering Jerry and chases him from the room. Jerry brings back three tough alley cats (featuring Meathead and the gang) who put Tom through a vigorous routine of baby life, completely wrecking Tom and the room while performing a Carmen Miranda-ish rendition of "Mama, Yo Quiero." When the little girl returns, Tom is punished with a baby-like dose of castor oil, as is the (formerly) laughing Jerry.

THE ZOOT CAT
Running Time 7.03 min. Release Date 26 Feb 1944

Tom tries to wow his hep cat girlfriend in a zoot suit fashioned from a hammock. Crooning and swooning, he simply dazzles the chick until Jerry interrupts his jitterbug routines, inheriting at tale's end both the suit and the girl.

THE MILLION DOLLAR CAT
Running Time 7.10 min. Release Date 6 May 1944

Tom inherits a million dollars from an eccentric relative, but a condition of the will reads that he "refrain from harming any living creature, including even a mouse." The cat who has everything moves to a penthouse and dines on silver salvers but can't get hold of an aggravating Jerry, who constantly reminds him of the condition of the will. Finally, the outraged Tom tears up the will and tears into Jerry, exclaiming, "I just threw away a million bucks, but I'm happy."

THE BODYGUARD
Running Time 7.21 min. Release Date 22 July 1944

When Jerry frees Spike from a city pound truck, the dog promises that if Jerry ever needs anything, all he has to do is "just whistle" for him. Tom sabotages the mouse's pucker with a piece of bubble gum. Unable to whistle, Jerry huffs and puffs and blows a huge bubble, which explodes with a bang. But too late: Spike has been recaptured by the pound, and Jerry is left running down the street, whistling.

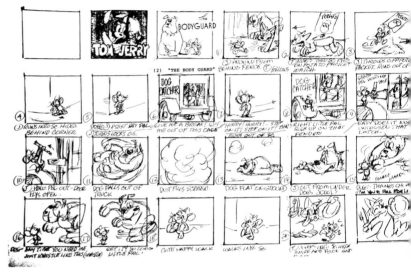

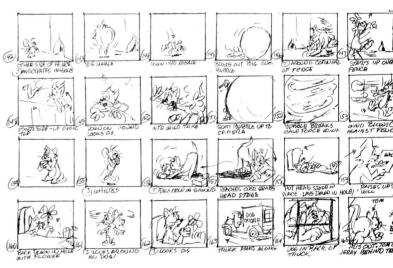

A storyboard for The Bodyguard.

In Mouse In Manhattan,
country mouse Jerry rubbernecks
at the skyscrapers of New York.
(Notice the twisted neck.)

Sailing along the gutter in a candy
wrapper raft, he expresses
perfectly the exhilaration of the
city.

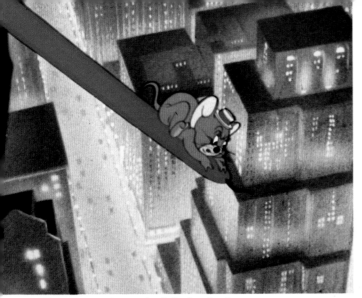

In a swanky nightclub, he climbs up on a candle for a peek at the skyline and finds himself with a better view than he had intended.

PUTTIN' ON THE DOG
Running Time 7.02 min. Release Date 28 Oct 1944

When Tom chases Jerry into the dog pound, he finds himself on dangerous turf. Cat tricks the canines by puttin' on a stuffed dog's head, but when Jerry runs away with it, he finds himself clinging to the top of a flagpole while the dogs bark viciously below.

MOUSE TROUBLE
Running Time 7.21 min. Release Date 23 Nov 1944

Reading the Random Mouse publication "How to Catch a Mouse," Tom uses every trick in the book to trap Jerry, but the wily mouse turns the tables every time. This cartoon snared the year's Oscar.

THE MOUSE COMES TO DINNER
Running Time 7.18 min. Release Date 5 May 1945

When Tom invites his kitten girlfriend to dinner, Jerry is pressed into service as a waiter, a corkscrew, and a lighter. But Tom's amorous advances have an adverse effect on the kitten, who flattens him with a hammer labeled "wolf pacifier." And when Jerry gets in on the act, cats and mouse have a three course free-for-all, ending with Tom christened the "S.S. Drip" and launched into the punch bowl to the tune of "Anchors Aweigh."

MOUSE IN MANHATTAN
Running Time 8.06 min. Release Date 7 July 1945

Country mouse Jerry takes a trip to the Big Apple where he admires the skyscrapers, stumbles into a powder room, dangles over the city on a candle, and dances in a nightclub. Confronted by an alleyful of hungry cats, shot at by police in a jewelry store window, and pursued by a subway train, he decides there's no place like home.

The country mouse has had his fill of adventures and leaves New York, chased by a subway train. Tom, at home asleep through the entire cartoon, appears only briefly (when Jerry leaves a "good-bye forever" note next to him and when he returns and joyfully kisses the somnolent cat, who didn't even know he was gone). The figure of Tom was added to this frame later for publicity purposes.

TEE FOR TWO
Running Time 7.00 min. *Release Date* 21 July 1945

On the golf links, Tom uses Jerry for a tee, and that's where the trouble begins. He hits a ball which ricochets off a tree, hitting him in the teeth. Jerry switches a ball for a woodpecker egg and the emerging bird homes in like a dive bomber, soon followed by a squadron of bees. Tom heads for underwater relief in the water hazard, but Jerry points out his location to the swarm.

FLIRTY BIRDY
Running Time 7.13 min. *Release Date* 22 Sept 1945

Tom is just about to eat a mouse sandwich when a hawk swoops down and saves little Jerry. Tom disguises himself as a lady hawk in order to get him back, but the feathered foe falls madly in love with him, and he can't get rid of the lovestruck bird.

QUIET PLEASE
Running Time 7.43 min. *Release Date* 22 Dec 1945

Tom's pursuit of Jerry awakens Spike, who warns Tom that if he makes one little noise, he'll skin him alive. Jerry takes the cue and makes every effort to wake the dog, finally succeeding with a firecracker. Spike does what every cartoon dog wants to do to a cat, and Tom finds himself bandaged head to toe, gently rocking a cradle with the sleeping Spike in it. This film quietly ran away with the year's Oscar.

SPRINGTIME FOR THOMAS
Running Time 7.37 min. *Release Date* 30 Mar 1946

On a beautiful spring day, Tom stares dreamily at a girl cat sunbathing in the next yard. Jerry breaks up the budding affair by sending a perfume-laced forged letter to Tom's adversary, slick, guitar-playing Meathead, and the race is on for the kitten's affections.

THE MILKY WAIF
Running Time 7.58 min. *Release Date* 18 May 1946

When baby mouse Nibbles (in his screen debut) is abandoned on Jerry's doorstep, it spells trouble for both Tom and Jerry. After a slight confusion about who to hit with the frying pan, Nibbles shows his mettle as Jerry's stalwart aide, and when Tom strikes little Nibbles with a flyswatter, Jerry turns into a roaring mighty mouse and rushes to his rescue.

TRAP HAPPY
Running Time 7.08 min. *Release Date* 29 June 1946

Tom calls in an exterminator (Meathead again, in a jaunty blue derby) to dispose of Jerry. But all his attempts, including cheese-scented perfume and dynamite, fail miserably, as clever Jerry sets his two pursuers against one another.

SOLID SERENADE

Running Time 7.21 min. Release Date 31 Mar 1946

Tom brings along his bass fiddle to serenade his girlfriend, but Spike is in the yard. Hampered by the bad-tempered dog and Jerry, Tom's crooning becomes his swan song as Jerry plays his whiskers for the pretty cat while Spike strums his tail.

CAT FISHIN'

Running Time 7.54 min. Release Date 22 Feb 1947

On a fishing trip, Tom uses Jerry as bait in order to catch a huge fish. But when Spike shows up, Jerry ties Tom's fishing line to the dog, and Tom reels in more than he had bargained for.

PART TIME PAL

Running Time 7.50 min. Release Date 15 Mar 1947

When Tom falls into a barrel of cider, the inebriated puss raids the refrigerator, pals up with Jerry, demolishes a cake, and tries to give Mammy a hot foot. But when he douses her with a pitcher of water, she chases the crazy cat out of the house and down the street.

THE CAT CONCERTO

Running Time 7.49 min. Release Date 26 Apr 1947

The audience has all the fun as Tom snootily accepts concert hall applause for his rendition of Liszt's Hungarian Rhapsody No. 2. But when Jerry turns "Rhapsody" into "On the Atchison, Topeka and the Santa Fe," all Tom can do is follow his lead. Things only get worse from here for the cat, but the cartoon won an Oscar for its classic combination of music and laughter.

DR. JEKYLL AND MR. MOUSE★

Running Time 7.24 min. Release Date 14 June 1947

Eerie atmospherics prevail as Jerry laps up a mixture of toxic liquids prepared by Tom and turns into a diabolical supersize supermouse. But when Tom drinks a new batch of the potion, he shrinks.

SALT WATER TABBY

Running Time 7.16 min. Release Date 12 July 1947

At the seashore, Tom woos a girl cat while Jerry munches on goodies inside the picnic basket. The beach battle begins, with Jerry putting an oyster in Tom's sandwich, salt in his coffee, and saltwater in his drink. At tale's end, with Tom high over the sand in a balloon, Jerry sails into the sunset on the picnic basket.

A MOUSE IN THE HOUSE

Running Time 7.49 min. Release Date 30 Aug 1947

Mammy warns layabouts Tom and Meathead that whichever of them fails to catch Jerry will go. The cats look everywhere, aided by Jerry himself, and in a very funny sequence with a gas oven and a match, end up, minus the mouse, in blackface. When Tom and Meathead paddle Mammy, each thinking she's the other, the housekeeper ejects both from the house, along with the mouse they were supposed to catch.

In Solid Serenade, *Jerry, pursued by Tom, has leaped into the kitchen sink, pulled the plug and strategically positioned himself on the window sill. Tom, crashing into the sink which now holds only (broken) dishes, has gone for the sill – much to his dismay.*

THE INVISIBLE MOUSE

Running Time 8.42 min. *Release Date* 27 Sept 1947

When Jerry lands in a bottle of invisible ink and discovers that he can't be seen, he sticks Tom's tail in a light socket, finishes the cat's milk just as he's about to drink it, and sets his toes on fire. The coup de grace occurs when the invisible mouse smashes a sleeping Spike with a golf club, leaving Tom to take the blame.

KITTY FOILED

Running Time 7.20 min. *Release Date* 1 June 1948

Jerry teams up with a canary to fight off Tom, but cat catches mouse and ties him to a toy train track. When Simon Legree Tom climbs into the engine and barrels down the track toward the helpless Jerry, the canary comes to the rescue, dropping a bowling ball from the air to create a deep hole into which the train plunges with Tom still aboard.

THE TRUCE HURTS

Running Time 7.59 min. *Release Date* 17 July 1948

Spike the bulldog decides to make amends with Tom and in turn Tom agrees to make peace with Jerry. When the trio comes upon a juicy steak, however, a cat-mouse-dog battle ensues over who is to have the largest piece.

OLD ROCKIN' CHAIR TOM

Running Time 7.39 min. *Release Date* 18 Sept 1948

Mammy replaces Tom with a ginger cat named Lightning, who lives up to his name in mouse catching. Tom and Jerry team up to disgrace the rival and save face for "old" Tom. Their tactics include a hilarious sequence in which they force Lightning to swallow an iron and then maneuver him about the room with a magnet. Tom "saves" Mammy from Jerry, and happily kicks Lightning out of his house.

PROFESSOR TOM

Running Time 7.47 min. *Release Date* 30 Oct 1948

Tom is teaching his student kitten how to catch a mouse when Jerry interrupts the class. The little cat, not the best scholar, pairs up with Jerry to knock out Tom. Between kitten and rodent, tutor Tom gets smoked out, crammed in the mailbox, and smacked with a bat, while the two chums romp off.

MOUSE CLEANING

Running Time 7.23 min. *Release Date* 11 Dec 1948

When Tom tracks mud into Mammy's freshly scoured house, she tells him he must restore its shine before she returns from the market. Jerry goes into high gear, throwing a tomato on the wall, dumping ink in Tom's cleaning water, spreading more ink on Tom's paws, and for the grand finale, letting loose a truckload of coal in the living-room.

POLKA DOT PUSS

Running Time 7.38 min. *Release Date* 26 Feb 1949

While Tom is asleep, Jerry paints his face with polka dots, convincing the cat he has measles. He naively puts himself in Jerry's hands for a rather creative course of nursing. After being frozen, baked and basted, Tom finally discovers the hoax, but also discovers that Jerry – and he – really do have measles.

THE LITTLE ORPHAN

Running Time 7.50 min. *Release Date* 30 Apr 1949[1]

Jerry kindly invites little orphan mouse Nibbles to Thanksgiving dinner and finds him a welcome ally in his continuing battle with Tom. The two join forces to elude the cat and eat the feast, until finally Tom waves the white flag of surrender. A fifth Oscar for Tom and Jerry, a first for Nibbles.

HATCH UP YOUR TROUBLES*

Running Time 7.50 min. *Release Date* 14 May 1949

When an egg finds its way into Jerry's bed and hatches there, the little mouse finds himself playing mama to a baby woodpecker. "Mama" mouse can't help when Tom swallows the little fellow, but it's Tom who's in trouble when Junior starts pecking his way out.

[1]The reader may note that the release date of this cartoon is 1949, while the film won its Oscar in 1948. Why? The cartoon was probably given a one day's run at a theater such as the Four Star on Wilshire Boulevard in Los Angeles in late 1948 in order to qualify for the Academy Award that year.

HEAVENLY PUSS
Running Time 7.48 min. *Release Date* 9 July 1949

In a delectable tale reminiscent of MGM's own *Heaven Can Wait*, Tom tries to gain entrance to the pearly gates but is turned away unless he can obtain a certificate of forgiveness from Jerry within an hour. The alternative being a hell run by a devil-red bulldog, Tom attempts to get the mouse's signature, which becomes a diabolical challenge.

THE CAT AND THE MERMOUSE
Running Time 7.49 min. *Release Date* 3 Sept 1949

Underwater adventures as Tom chases Jerry beneath the sea, replete with sea horses, swordfish, and an octopus which ensnares Tom in his arms.

LOVE THAT PUP
Running Time 7.55 min. *Release Date* 1 Oct 1949

Tom and Jerry's perpetual chase leads them smack into the path of little Pup and his adoring, if overprotective father, Butch (aka Tyke and Spike). Butch warns Tom never to come near his son again – so Jerry stays close by. Tom can't resist temptation, however, and Pup becomes the pawn in a game of dog vs. cat vs. mouse.

JERRY'S DIARY
Running Time 6.43 min. *Release Date* 22 Oct 1949

This is the first of several wrap-around films, in which the story device (in this case, the diary) becomes a showcase for highlights from earlier cartoons. Here, Tom finds Jerry's diary, furiously reads of all the tricks Jerry has played on him (ignoring the ones he's played in return), and heaves a pie at the astonished mouse.

TENNIS CHUMPS
Running Time 6.49 min. *Release Date* 10 Dec 1949

Tom and cat foe Meathead play an aggressive game of tennis complete with iron and bomb balls supplied by ball mouse Jerry. When the two players violently collide at center court, their wrath turns to Jerry who sets up a ball machine to pelt the two attackers. At cartoon's end, the cat pros are up a tree and Jerry accepts the trophy.

LITTLE QUACKER
Running Time 7.07 min. *Release Date* 7 Jan 1950

In his screen debut, Quacker, a little yellow duckling, is nabbed by Tom. He escapes, finds a protector in Jerry, and the two elude the cat, until a climactic finish with a lawnmower and Papa Duck puts an end to Tom's dreams of roast duckling.

SATURDAY EVENING PUSS
Running Time 6.18 min. *Release Date* 14 Jan 1950

When Mammy goes out for the evening, Tom and his cat pals Shorty and Meathead hold a raucous party. Although they think it's the cat's meow, the turned-up tones of "Darktown Strutter's Ball" disturb Jerry's sleep. Terrific animation has Jerry's head changing configuration with every loud beat of music. He phones Mammy, who returns home, boots out the cats, and then, to his dismay, turns up the volume on the same loud tune.

TEXAS TOM
Running Time 6.34 min. *Release Date* 11 Mar 1950

This is an absolute gem of a cartoon. Tom, with all the smooth moves of the silver screen cowboy, lassoes Jerry and sings country-western songs to a li'l gal cat. But thanks to Jerry, he also ropes a bull, which flattens the aspiring cowboy. Jerry picks him up and triumphantly rides Tom into the sunset.

JERRY AND THE LION
Running Time 7.13 min. *Release Date* 8 Apr 1950

Jerry hides an escaped lion from a citywide search party, and Tom, in a pith helmet, goes on a house-wide safari in search of both. Jerry then sees the lion off on the S.S. Africa, tearfully waving goodbye.

SAFETY SECOND

Running Time 7.07 min. *Release Date* 1 July 1950

Jerry and Nibbles celebrate the Fourth of July. Nibbles wants fireworks; Jerry keeps trying to tell him they're dangerous. But when Tom intervenes, he finds they're rather useful after all, launching the cat into a star-spangled grand finale.

TOM AND JERRY IN THE HOLLYWOOD BOWL

Running Time 7.22 min. *Release Date* 16 Sept 1950

Tom is doing fine conducting an all-cat symphony orchestra in the overture to "Die Fledermaus" until Jerry decides he's going to do the conducting. Tom tries to throw him off the stage; Jerry retaliates by disposing of the orchestra members, one by one, until only Tom is left to play all the instruments while the mouse conducts.

THE FRAMED CAT

Running Time 7.11 min. *Release Date* 21 Oct 1950

Spike sternly warns Tom to stay away from his bone, so Jerry keeps planting it on the unsuspecting cat. Jerry places a magnet in Tom's mouth and a bit of iron in the coveted bone, then becomes part of the chase when he unwittingly jumps into a trash can sensitive to the magnet's pull.

CUE BALL CAT

Running Time 7.02 min. *Release Date* 25 Nov 1950

A snappy game of billiards results when Tom wakes Jerry from a nap on the pool table. Using the mouse as a billiard ball, the pool shark cat tries some fancy moves, but Jerry gets even with him when he places a hatpin in the top of the cue. Tom tries to hold his own, but by game's end, the balls are not in the pool table pockets but in Tom's mouth.

CASANOVA CAT

Running Time 7.04 min. *Release Date* 6 Jan 1951

Tom offers Jerry as a gift to Toodles, a wealthy female feline he's trying to impress. But the mouse calls on Meathead and while the two Lotharios vie for the lady's favor, Jerry ties their tails together and takes off by auto with the object of their desires.

JERRY AND THE GOLDFISH

Running Time 7.21 min. *Release Date* 3 Mar 1951

Cuisine à la cat as Tom tries to cook Goldy, the goldfish. Not to fear – Jerry's on hand to thwart the plans of the cavalier chef. When Tom puts the little fish in a pressure cooker, Jerry substitutes a stick of dynamite for a carrot and the cat ends up sky high.

JERRY'S COUSIN★

Running Time 6.39 min. *Release Date* 7 Apr 1951

Muscles, Jerry's cat-curdling cousin, arrives to help get Tom under control. In a derby hat and an oversized t-shirt, Muscles is a mean streets mouse, and more than a match for Tom. When a regime of body building fails, Tom calls in his alley cat friends, "Dirty Work, Inc." to rid the house of the miniature menace. But Muscles evicts them, too, and Tom gives in to his superior strength.

SLEEPY-TIME TOM

Running Time 7.05 min. *Release Date* 26 May 1951

After a night out with the boys, Tom is too exhausted to mouse hunt, which doesn't go over well with Mammy. Jerry entices him into the bedroom for a little illicit napping, but Mammy spots him and throws him through the window, where he's picked up by his pals for another night out.

HIS MOUSE FRIDAY

Running Time 7.11 min. *Release Date* 7 July 1951

Lost at sea on a life raft, Tom is washed ashore by a gigantic wave and meets up with Jerry, posing as a cannibal. When Robinson Crusoe cat uncovers the mouse's disguise, a band of real cannibals appears and the head hunters head for a nice meal of cat and mouse.

SLICKED-UP PUP

Running Time 6.19 min. *Release Date* 8 Sept 1951

Butch has just bathed Pup when Tom accidentally gets the little dog muddy while chasing Jerry. Dad orders the frightened cat to clean Pup or else, and with Jerry's "assistance" the little dog ends up painted, tarred and feathered. When Butch sees his son, he tosses Tom in the washing machine.

NIT-WITTY KITTY

Running Time 6.33 min. Release Date 6 Oct 1951

When Mammy whacks Tom with her broom, he suffers an attack of amnesia and begins acting like a mouse. Jerry, exasperated with having a giant buddy who eats his cheese, invades his mousehole, and sleeps in his bed (and breaks it), tries in vain to shake Tom out of his delusion. Finally, an ironing board falls on Tom's head and straightens him out, but Mammy strikes him on the head again, and he goes back to happy mousehood.

CAT NAPPING

Running Time 6.52 min. Release Date 8 Dec 1951

A lazy afternoon, a cool glass of lemonade, and Jerry snoozing in a hammock – until Tom decides he wants it. A battle for possession ensues, with Tom enlisting an army of ants and Jerry calling Spike into the fray.

THE FLYING CAT

Running Time 6.44 min. Release Date 12 Jan 1952

Jerry and a canary save one another from Tom's attack and take refuge in a birdhouse. Tom fashions a pair of wings from a girdle and flies after the canary, who leads Tom into a train tunnel. The cat soon finds himself suspended from a trestle as Jerry and the canary wave goodbye from a passing observation car.

Tom and Tuffy in another PR shot. You can tell at a glance that it's Tuffy and not Jerry simply by his stance.

THE DUCK DOCTOR

Running Time 7.03 min. *Release Date* 16 Feb 1952

Hunting in the woods, Tom wounds a duckling, little Quacker, who is doctored by Jerry. Hunter becomes the hunted as duck and mouse go after the cat, finally flattening him with a handy anvil.

THE TWO MOUSEKETEERS

Running Time 7.21 min. *Release Date* 15 Mar 1952

Given the responsibility of guarding the grand banquet table, Tom is confronted with the sudden appearance of mouseketeers Jerry and Tuffy. But the mice outwit the cat, turning the banquet table into a battlefield. Tom gets the guillotine while the mouseketeers march happily away munching on their spoils. Another Oscar for the swashbuckling trio.

SMITTEN KITTEN

Running Time 7.49 min. *Release Date* 12 Apr 1952

Another "wrap-around" cartoon, in which Tom is smitten by yet another kitten, provides the impetus for a series of flashbacks to other amorous misadventures. At the cartoon's end, Jerry meets a girl mouse and the little green devil who's been egging him on finds a mate, too.

TRIPLET TROUBLE
Running Time 7.09 min. *Release Date* 19 Apr 1952

Mammy babysits three seemingly sweet kittens who turn out to be little rascals. Taking on Tom, and then Jerry, is more than the hooligan trio bargains for, though, and tale's end finds them with bottoms glowing bright red from the spanking Jerry has given them.

LITTLE RUNAWAY
Running Time 7.04 min. *Release Date* 14 June 1952

A baby seal, escapee from the circus, is befriended by Jerry. Tom plans to return him for the large reward offered and disguises himself as a seal to lure him away from his mouse chum. But the boys from the big top pick up Tom instead and he finds himself performing in the next show.

FIT TO BE TIED
Running Time 6.49 min. *Release Date* 26 July 1952

When the mayor puts a new leash law into effect, Jerry's protector Spike is tied to his dog house. Tom takes undue advantage of both dog and mouse until the law is revoked. Now the roles are reversed, and it's Jerry and Spike's turn to leash Tom.

PUSH-BUTTON KITTY
Running Time 6.33 min. *Release Date* 6 Sept 1952

Mammy gets a mechanical cat which proves its superior mouse catching abilities by immediately evicting Jerry. The former house mouse releases an army of mechanical mice; "Mechano" tears up the place chasing them, until he self-destructs. Mammy, in her last screen appearance, is thankful to have Tom back on duty until he too makes a mess trying to catch the mechanical mice.

Jerry, disguised as an explosive white mouse, causes trouble for Tom in The Missing Mouse. *The brown mouse (who looks just like Jerry) was added to this publicity shot.*

CRUISE CAT

Running Time 7.02 min. *Release Date* 18 Oct 1952

As mascot aboard a Honolulu bound cruiser, Tom is warned by the captain that he'll be replaced if one single mouse is found aboard. Stowaway Jerry makes life miserable for Tom, who winds up in the brig, watching as Jerry rides ashore on a surfboard, strumming a ukelele.

THE DOG HOUSE

Running Time 6.39 min. *Release Date* 29 Nov 1952

In a variation on *Mr. Blandings Builds His Dream House*, Spike's building the doghouse of his dreams, but the unending chase between Tom and Jerry destroys it even when he tries putting it in a tree.

THE MISSING MOUSE

Running Time 6.33 min. *Release Date* 10 Jan 1953

Radio reports warn that a white mouse, having escaped from a lab, has swallowed enough explosive to blow up the city. The already terrified Tom mistakes Jerry, who has been dunked with white shoe polish, for the radical rodent, and Jerry has a gay old time taking advantage of the cat. The real white mouse appears, but Tom, hearing that the explosive has lost its potency, attacks the little rodent and the explosion destroys *only* a city block.

JERRY AND JUMBO

Running Time 7.13 min. *Release Date* 21 Feb 1953

More circus fun when a baby elephant falls from a passing train and into Tom's basket. Jerry helps hide the elephant by painting him up as a giant mouse, but Tom holds his own until mama pachyderm appears.

JOHANN MOUSE

Running Time 7.57 min. *Release Date* 21 Mar 1953

In the house of Johann Strauss is little Johann mouse, who loves to waltz. Tom, a piano playing cat, tries to catch him as he dances. When the emperor hears of this talented duo, he insists they perform before the royal party. This charming little film, with its storybook setting, marks the final Oscar for Tom and Jerry.

THAT'S MY PUP

Running Time 7.23 min. *Release Date* 25 Apr 1953

Spike is teaching his son Tyke how to chase cats just as Tom appears, chasing Jerry. Tyke and Jerry take turns barking at Tom, until the cat, figuring out the score, posts Tyke to the top of a flagpole. Then Spike returns.

JUST DUCKY

Running Time 7.57 min. *Release Date* 5 Sept 1953

Jerry tries to teach little Quacker to swim. Tom sees him as duck soup and tries to cook him. But when Tom almost drowns, the little duck bravely rescues him and Tom and Jerry proudly watch their little friend swim away.

TWO LITTLE INDIANS

Running Time 6.49 min. *Release Date* 17 Oct 1953

Scoutmaster Jerry has his hands full with two little orphans from the Bide A Wee Mouse Home. Outfitted in Indian feathers and diapers, the two involve Jerry and the sleeping Spike in a hair-raising battle with Tom. The cat, in a Davy Crockett coonskin cap, fights valiantly, but finally gives in and sits down to smoke the peace pipe with the wild Indians.

LIFE WITH TOM

Running Time 7.49 min. *Release Date* 21 Nov 1953

Third of the "wrap-arounds" that Hanna and Barbera directed, this cartoon has Tom embarrassed by the contents of Jerry's best selling book, "Life with Tom." Just as he's about to hit Jerry over the head with a copy of the book, Jerry tells him that half of the royalty check goes to him. Tom's embarrassment turns to sheer glee.

PUPPY TALE

Running Time 7.03 min. *Release Date* 23 Jan 1954

Jerry rescues a sackful of puppies from a storm swollen river, and one of them follows him home. Tom, not wanting anything to do with dogs, throws pup and mouse into the rainy night. But the cat's heart softens and when he goes after them into the storm, he falls in the river and almost drowns.

Rescued by Jerry and the puppy, he soon finds himself surrounded by the pup's five siblings.

POSSE CAT
Running Time 6.28 min. Release Date 30 Jan 1954

The ranch cook tells Tom that if he doesn't throw Jerry out of the cook shack he won't get any dinner. Cat and mouse arrange a fake shooting scene to make Tom a hero; Jerry is to get half of Tom's dinner. But Tom doublecrosses Jerry who, in turn, exposes the varmint, resulting in a well-fed Jerry and a fleeing Tom.

HIC-CUP PUP
Running Time 6.17 min. Release Date 17 Apr 1954

This puppy tale finds Tyke being set down for a nap by Papa Spike. But continual interruption by Tom and Jerry results in a case of hiccups for the pup. ("Every time his sleep gets distoibed, he gets the hiccups," explains Spike.) And for Pop. ("I'll moider that – hiccup – cat," Spike adds.) But Tom inadvertently saves the day by scaring the hiccups out of father and son.

LITTLE SCHOOL MOUSE
Running Time 7.50 min. Release Date 29 May 1954

In the flip side of *Professor Tom*, Jerry teaches little Tuffy the art of outwitting a cat. Tuffy is a brilliant

pupil and shows his teacher a few new tricks, much to Jerry's chagrin. At the story's end, Tom, and Jerry in a dunce cap, are Tuffy's pupils, learning that cats and mice should be friends.

BABY BUTCH
Running Time 7.09 min. Release Date 14 Mar 1954

Butch (shaggy alley cat Meathead) dresses in baby togs and leaves himself on Tom's doorstep as a means of gaining entry to the icebox. Jerry teams up with Tom to foil the sham baby's plans and Butch gets the boot.

MICE FOLLIES
Running Time 6.49 min. Release Date 4 Sept 1954

Jerry and Tuffy turn the kitchen floor into a skating rink by freezing water into a solid sheet of ice. Tom goes after the two ice-skating mice, but he's no match for the agile pair and comes out on the short end of the struggle for the ice-rink.

NEAPOLITAN MOUSE
Running Time 7.15 min. Release Date 2 Oct 1954

Touring Naples, Tom and Jerry are befriended by Italian mouse Topo, a champion of justice who helps his new friends fight off some tough Italian dogs. Cat and mice are victorious as the dogs are hit by large Italian cheeses which send them into the Bay of Naples.

DOWNHEARTED DUCKLING
Running Time 6.42 min. Release Date 13 Nov 1954

Quacker reads "The Ugly Duckling" and convinced he's ugly, too, tries to get Tom to eat him. Tom, only too happy to oblige, is foiled every time by Jerry. The mouse then attempts a beauty make-over program, but meets with no success. But when Quacker meets a girl duck who thinks he's cute, he happily takes her arm and they waddle off together.

The studio caption for this "portrait" read: "Bachrat, famous photographer of furry celebrities the world over, is credited by Tom & Jerry for this photograph, said to stand paw and tail over all others."

PET PEEVE
Running Time 6.35 min. *Release Date* 20 Nov 1954

Husband and wife tell Tom and Spike that, due to the high cost of feeding them, one must go, and the one who catches Jerry will stay. In their frantic efforts to trap him, they cut up everything from the carpet to the master's slippers. Both are thrown out of the house, and Jerry becomes the new pet – after all, a mouse doesn't eat very much (?).

TOUCHE, PUSSY CAT★
Running Time 6.45 min. *Release Date* 18 Dec 1954

Tuffy's father sends him to Jerry for mouseketeer training, but the little fellow fails badly, exuberantly slicing up everything in Jerry's apartment and poking him with his sword. But, just as Jerry is sending him home in disgrace, Tuffy comes to the rescue when Tom attacks, and wins the coveted title of mouseketeer after all.

SOUTHBOUND DUCKLING
Running Time 6.15 min. *Release Date* 12 Mar 1955

Stubborn Quacker, convinced this time that all ducks go south for the winter, refuses to stay home like his domestic buddies even though he can't fly. To complicate matters, Tom is reading "How to Cook a Duck." After repeated rescues of Quacker, Jerry flies with him (by airplane) to Florida, where Tom meets up with them.

A publicity still of that favorite father and son, Spike and Tyke.

PUP ON A PICNIC
Running Time 7.04 min. *Release Date* 30 Apr 1955

Jerry hides in Spike and Tyke's picnic basket to escape from Tom, who invites himself along. More food fight fun as Spike, Tom, and Jerry vie over the contents of the basket. At cartoon's end, Jerry is borne away on a sandwich litter by a parade of hungry ants.

MOUSE FOR SALE
Running Time 6.48 min. *Release Date* 21 May 1955

White mice being the new rage, Tom paints Jerry white with the idea of selling him for a tidy profit. His plan works until the lady of the house returns with her new purchase, Jerry. Tom attacks Jerry, now considered a "dancing mouse," and is locked out of the house until he paints himself white and dances his way back in.

DESIGNS ON JERRY
Running Time 6.39 min. *Release Date* 2 Sept 1955

How to build the ultimate mousetrap: Tom blueprints an extremely elaborate design. But the drawn sketch comes to life, tells Jerry about Tom's plan, and together they change a few critical dimensions. Tom builds the trap according to the altered plans and becomes the victim of his own ingenuity.

TOM AND CHERIE
Running Time 6.46 min. *Release Date* 9 Sept 1955

Another entry in the mouseketeers series. Jerry sends Tuffy as a special messenger to his ladylove. But each time, poor Tuffy must get past the devilish Tom, and each time he returns more tattered than the last. But when he tires of the cat's harassment and simply refuses to fight, Tom lets him pass unharmed.

SMARTY CAT
Running Time 6.50 min. *Release Date* 14 Oct 1955

The last "wrap-around" entry directed by Hanna and Barbera. When Tom and his cat pals show their home movies, Jerry brings Spike over to peek through the window. The dog sees himself depicted as a big goof, breaks into the screening, rips the

equipment apart, and takes off after the three cats. Now Jerry has some interesting home movies of his own, having filmed the entire scuffle with his little movie camera.

PECOS PEST

Running Time 6.35 min. Release Date 11 Nov 1955

Jerry's Uncle Pecos spends an evening with his nephew just before his scheduled television appearance and finds that Tom's whiskers make fine guitar strings. As Pecos performs on TV, one of his strings breaks and, to the cat's amazement, Pecos reaches out of the television set, yanks out Tom's remaining whisker, and continues his performance.

THAT'S MY MOMMY

Running Time 6.03 min. Release Date 19 Nov 1955

Hatching at Tom's feet, little Quacker thinks the cat is his "dear sweet Mommy." Tom's main interest is still how to cook a duck. But after Jerry foils his plan several times, the cat's conscience finally gets the better of him, and he leads Quacker across the duck pond, warmly quacking to his "son" as any good mother should.

THE FLYING SORCERESS

Running Time 6.40 min. Release Date 27 Jan 1956

Tom unsuspectingly takes a new job with a witch. He steals her broom to return to home and scares the wits out of Jerry. Suddenly Tom awakens, realizes that he's been dreaming, and experiments with a real broom, which suddenly takes off, sending him sailing toward the moon.

THE EGG AND JERRY

Running Time 7.50 min. Release Date 23 Mar 1956

A CinemaScope remake of *Hatch Up Your Troubles* (1949).

BUSY BUDDIES

Running Time 6.15 min. Release Date 4 May 1956

A prequel to *Tot Watchers*, this cartoon concerns Jeannie, the babysitter whose prime interest is the telephone, and a baby whose main interest is crawling into mischief. Tom and Jerry rescue him from the sink, the curtain rod, the basement and the mailbox down the street, only to be accused of bothering the baby.

MUSCLE BEACH TOM

Running Time 6.45 min. Release Date 7 Sept 1956

Butch, Tom's cat pal, impresses the girl they both want, with awesome displays of weight lifting. Jealous Tom tries for the well-muscled look by stuffing his bathing suit with balloons, but Jerry unties him from his beach umbrella anchor, and Tom floats away.

DOWNBEAT BEAR

Running Time 6.22 min. Release Date 21 Oct 1956

A dancing bear who has escaped from the circus uses the reluctant Tom for his dancing partner, giving Jerry trouble-free access to the icebox.

BLUE CAT BLUES

Running Time 6.48 min. Release Date 16 Nov 1956

When Tom loses his girlfriend to arch rival Butch again, it's too much and he ends up on the railroad tracks, pondering suicide. When Jerry loses his girl-friend, he joins Tom on the tracks.

BARBECUE BRAWL

Running Time 6.34 min. Release Date 14 Dec 1956

Spike's perfect poolside barbecue turns into a dis-aster when Tom and Jerry crash the cookout. Steak, salad and bread are in turn demolished, and an ant army runs away with what's left.

TOPS WITH POPS

Running Time 7.55 min. Release Date 22 Feb 1957

This is a CinemaScope remake of *Love That Pup* (1949).

TIMID TABBY

Running Time 6.49 min. Release Date 19 Apr 1957

Tom's cousin, George, a fraidy cat, has a mouse phobia. When he comes to visit, Tom assures him there are no mice in the house. But Jerry is in the house, and every time George sees him, he runs away, causing the little mouse to become increas-ingly braver . . . until he sees both Tom and his cousin together.

FEEDIN' THE KIDDIE

Running Time 7.40 min. Release Date 7 June 1957

A CinemaScope remake of *The Little Orphan* (1949).

MUCHO MOUSE

Running Time 7.04 min. Release Date 6 Sept 1957

Tom, the "Olympic, U.S. and World Champion Mouse Catcher," goes to Spain to try to catch "El Magnifico" (Jerry), who foils all of the champion cat's attacks. Meathead has a cameo role.

TOM'S PHOTO FINISH

Running Time 6.19 min. Release Date 1 Nov 1957

Tom frames Spike for stealing food from the refri-gerator, but Jerry takes a photo of the perfidious puss in the act. When Jerry stuffs copies of the photo in a newspaper and a cake and turns another into a paper airplane, Tom has his hands full trying to keep his master and mistress from finding them.

HAPPY GO DUCKY

Running Time 6.24 min. Release Date 3 Jan 1958

When the Easter Bunny leaves an egg for Tom and Jerry, it's no piece of candy. The egg hatches into Quacker, who insists on swimming in everything in the house from the fishbowl to the bathtub. Finally flooding the house with water, he calls in four duck friends, who paddle around the living-room singing "Happy Easter."

ROYAL CAT NAP

Running Time 6.45 min. Release Date 7 Mar 1958

In the fourth, and last, mouseketeers entry, unruly swashbucklers Jerry and Tuffy wake the king, who warns his servant Tom that if his sleep is interrupted again, he'll lose his head. When the mice reawaken the monarch, Tuffy sings him back to sleep with "Frère Jacques" and saves Tom's head.

Animator's sketches of Tom and Jerry in action, done specially for this book by Irv Spence.

THE VANISHING DUCK

Running Time 7.04 min. Release Date 2 May 1958

Quacker, in his last Tom & Jerry film, plays a sing-ing duck who becomes Jerry's partner in crime when the two of them discover the delights of vanishing cream. Thus invisible, they gleefully bamboozle poor Tom, until he too learns the secret.

ROBIN HOODWINKED

Running Time 6.15 min. Release Date 6 June 1958

Daring mice Jerry and Tuffy decide to break Robin Hood out of prison, but must first get by guard Tom. Tuffy is able to get the key for Robin's cell by pulling it from Tom's mouth while the cat sleeps. The mice then knock Tom out with a mace and successfully free Robin and his men. This film marks Tuffy's last appearance.

TOT WATCHERS

Running Time 6.28 min. Release Date 1 Aug 1958

Babysitter Jeannie, still infatuated with the telephone, once again leaves Tom and Jerry minding the baby. When the tot crawls out of the house and onto a dangerous construction site, Tom and Jerry rescue him, only to be arrested for baby-snatching.

Irv Spence demonstrates drawing Tom during a recent interview at his home.

137

THE GENE DEITCH YEARS

SWITCHIN' KITTEN
Running Time 8.40 min. Release Date 7 Sept 1961

In an eerie castle, Jerry is a mad scientist's assistant and Tom is his unwilling subject. When Tom is changed into a dog and the dog into a cat, it's only the beginning of role reversal problems for all.

DOWN AND OUTING
Running Time 6.49 min. Release Date 26 Oct 1961

A day of fishing turns out to be more than Tom, Jerry or their master had angled for. Before they've even arrived, a battle takes place in the car for who will complete the trip – and all that gets left on the road is burnt rubber and the master's nerves. Once on board the boat, Tom tosses Jerry in the water and the mouse retaliates by tying Tom's hook to the master's foot.

IT'S GREEK TO ME-OW
Running Time 6.46 min. Release Date 7 Dec 1961

Toga-clad Tom and Jerry are at it again in ancient Athens. Tom, hot on Jerry's trail, tries to gain entrance to a "no cats allowed" club. Thrown out by a guard, he disguises himself with a statue's head and sneaks back in. But when he ends up in a runaway chariot, it spells the ancient Greek end for Tom.

HIGH STEAKS
Running Time 6.21 min. Release Date Jan 1962

Backyard barbecue fun as Tom and his master, grill steaks near the pool. But when Jerry arrives, it's a free for all as he scorches Tom's tail, engages him in a fencing match with forks, and sends the master into a rage over a bottle of Kooky Kola.

MOUSE INTO SPACE
Running Time 6.34 min. Release Date Feb 1962

Jerry enlists in the Astro-Mouse Program to elude Tom but finds the cat aboard his space capsule. Summarily ejected, Tom streaks across the stars, encountering a cosmonaut pooch and cache of meteorites before falling to earth.

LANDING STRIPLING
Running Time 6.18 min. Release Date Apr 1962

Tom, trying to lure a flying bird, makes a landing strip from Christmas lights to signal in his prey. But an airliner swoops down instead, carrying Tom into the sky.

CALYPSO CAT
Running Time 7.50 min. Release Date June 1962

Tom falls for a Persian cat whom he and Jerry join for a Caribbean cruise aboard a luxury liner. But Tom's ideas of island romance are ruined when the Persian scornfully leaves him for a calypso cat.

DICKY MOE
Running Time 7.05 min. Release Date July 1962

In a twist on the classic *Moby Dick*, Tom is press-ganged aboard the ship of a mad captain obsessed with the whale Dicky Moe. Made to scrub the decks, Tom gets unhelpful assistance from Jerry, who substitutes tar for water. When Dicky Moe is sighted, the captain fires a cannon at him, and the whale takes off, with Tom roped to his side.

THE TOM AND JERRY CARTOON KIT
Running Time 6.28 min. Release Date Aug 1962

The Tom and Jerry cartoon kit is rather simple – just the cat and mouse and an assortment of deadly weapons. The forever-battling duo go through a couple of combat examples and, as the narrator tells of further cartoon possibilities, Jerry puts the lid on the kit, trapping Tom inside.

TALL IN THE TRAP
Running Time 7.49 min. Release Date Sept 1962

When Jerry steals cheese from the Dry Gulp General Store, the sheriff hires Tom, the fastest trap in the West, but Jerry tricks him into blowing up the sheriff's office. The lawman chases Tom out of town and Jerry takes off with more cheese.

SORRY SAFARI
Running Time 7.17 min. Release Date Oct 1962

On safari in darkest Africa, Tom and Jerry join their master on a "Nertz" rent-an-elephant. The master finds once again that travels with Tom and Jerry can be difficult (when he is charged by a lion, he finds that Tom has replaced his gun with a thermos bottle). At tale's end, the elephant and Jerry are carrying the spoils of the hunt – Tom, the master and a rhino – tied to a pole.

BUDDIES THICKER THAN WATER

Running Time 8.58 min. *Release Date* Nov 1962

Jerry, sleeping in a Tiffany's box in a penthouse, takes freezing, starving Tom into his home. But when the mistress of the house tries to evict the cat, he scares her with Jerry and perfidiously tosses him out into the snow. Pampered by the grateful woman, Tom is haunted by "ghost" Jerry and flees outside to freeze again.

CARMEN GET IT!

Running Time 7.38 min. *Release Date* Dec 1962

Jerry runs into the Metropolitan Opera, trying to evade Tom. The cat disguises himself as a violinist, with a tape recorder hidden in his fiddle. But Jerry plays it in reverse and the conductor breaks the offending instrument over Tom's head. When Tom conducts the orchestra, Jerry sends a score of ants scurrying onto his music sheets, and poor Tom has a hard time differentiating the bugs from the notes.

Jerry is rudely awakened by opera star Tom singing onstage just above his head in The Cat Above and The Mouse Below.

THE CHUCK JONES YEARS

PENTHOUSE MOUSE

Running Time 7.08 min. *Release Date* 1963

The luxurious life of Tom, a penthouse puss, goes to the dogs after poor mouse Jerry falls from a construction site onto his terrace. A wild chase ensues and Tom ends up pursued by the entrants in the nearby National Dog Show, while Jerry gets used to a life of luxury on the 50th floor.

THE CAT ABOVE AND THE MOUSE BELOW

Running Time 6.27 min. *Release Date* 1964

Tom, famous baritone Signor Thomasino Catti-Cazzaza, enthralls a concert audience with his rendition of "Rigoletto" while Jerry strives for sleep under the stage. When mouse attempts to stop cat, it's a case of basso buffo until Tom ends up beneath the floor and Jerry finishes the concert.

IS THERE A DOCTOR IN THE MOUSE?

Running Time 7.13 min. *Release Date* 1964

Jerry mixes and drinks a high accceleration potion which renders him so fast that he eats all of Tom's food before the bewildered cat can even see him. Tom tries various traps but Jerry's too quick for them all. Filming the food theft and developing it in his darkroom, Tom identifies the thief and pulls Jerry out of his mousehole, only to discover that, with his next elixir, he's grown giant-sized.

In Is There A Doctor in the Mouse? *Jerry drinks his own concoction, which gives him lightning speed and agility. In this scene, he's just taken the potion and is looking rather greedily toward his next meal.*

Tom tries to evict a kitten who's taken over his turf in The Unshrinkable Jerry Mouse.

MUCH ADO ABOUT MOUSING
Running Time 6.38 min.   Release Date 1964

When a bulldog tells Jerry to "just whistle" any time he needs him, Tom's in for big trouble until he puts earmuffs on the mutt.

SNOWBODY LOVES ME
Running Time 7.48 min.   Release Date 1964

Waif mouse Jerry, encrusted with snow, peers through a warmly lit window at Tom asleep by the fire in a room full of cheese. Once in the house, Jerry jumps into a wheel of swiss and proceeds to make himself at home. Tom stops up all the holes and blows up the cheese, pelting himself with corks. Jerry, finding himself cheeseless and in a cheese-slice tutu, performs a delicate ballet.

THE UNSHRINKABLE JERRY MOUSE
Running Time 6.45 min.   Release Date 1964

Tom enjoys the role of top cat until an adorable kitten is brought into the house. Resenting the little cat's presence, Tom tries to get rid of him, but Jerry is always there to foil his plans. At story's end, Jerry and the kitten are comfortably ensconced in Tom's basket while the cat rubs the sly little mouse's neck.

AH, SWEET MOUSE-STORY OF LIFE
Running Time 6.00 min.   Release Date 1965

In a trip into the abstract, Jerry, chased by Tom and falling through the air, grabs onto a question mark and floats gently to the ground while the cat grabs an exclamation point and plummets like a stone.

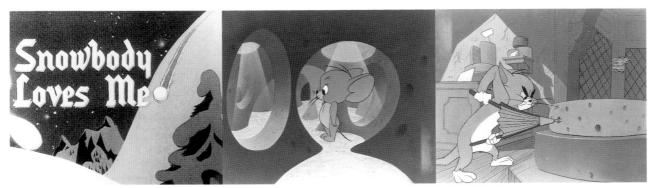

Scenes from Chuck Jones'
Snowbody Loves Me. *The snowball caroming down the mountain is Jerry. Having found his way into Tom's cozy house, he makes himself at home in a wheel of swiss cheese. But Tom evicts him from his new abode, and Jerry, emerging from his blown up home in a cheese tutu, can't resist dancing the ballet. Tom throws him back out into the snow and, snuggly warm in his blanket by the fire, his conscience gets the better of him. The cat retrieves the little mouse from the cold, and happily plays pianop accompaniment to his Bavarian polka.*

In the opening scene of The Brothers Carry-Mouse-Off, *Jerry is sunning himself poolside when his radar warns him of Tom's approach.* Right: *Jerry fishes with a plunger in* The Brothers Carry-Mouse-Off.

TOM-IC ENERGY
Running Time 6.40 min. *Release Date* 1965

Jerry leads Tom through fire escapes, rooftops and manholes in staying just a step ahead of the contentious cat. Tom smashes into a passing bulldog and is temporarily derailed until Jerry rescues him and the chase is resumed.

BAD DAY AT CAT ROCK
Running Time 6.15 min. *Release Date* 1965

In a titular reference to MGM's own *Bad Day at Black Rock*, it's a bad day for poor Tom. First Jerry lures him into a dark manhole where a stash of TNT explodes, then the rascally mouse puts on a huge rubber glove and boxes the confused cat. Jerry arms himself with a can of paint and takes advantage of Tom, pinned under a rock, by painting "The End" on it.

THE BROTHERS CARRY-MOUSE-OFF
Running Time 6.27 min. *Release Date* 1965

Another MGM film (and Dostoevsky novel), *The Brothers Karamazov*, provided the title for this outing. Here, Tom's efforts to entice Jerry to him with

142

food are defeated before they're begun, for the mouse picks him up on his special poolside radar. Tom then dons a mouse costume and squirts himself with eau de mouse, attracting first a whole swarm of mice, and then a group of neighborhood cats.

HAUNTED MOUSE
Running Time 6.49 min. Release Date 1965

Jerry, with the top hat and cloak of a stage magician and the powers of a real wizard, makes life miserable for poor Tom, who temporarily loses his nose to the tiny sorcerer. And while Jerry dines with his mouse girlfriend, Tom is clobbered by rabbits that jump from Jerry's magic hat.

I'M JUST WILD ABOUT JERRY
Running Time 6.39 min. Release Date 1965

Tom knocks Jerry off his roller skates and eventually onto a ping pong table, where he volleys the little mouse. Jerry grabs a mallet and sends a very alarmed Tom down an elevator shaft, out of the building, and onto a railroad track on which a train is rapidly approaching. But angelic Jerry, replete with wings and halo, switches the tracks at the last second and the train speeds harmlessly past.

Jerry hides in a toy mouse line-up in I'm Just Wild About Jerry. *Tom tugs on the tail of each to find the real rodent.*

In another scene from I'm Just Wild About Jerry, *the title mouse acts the unwilling ping pong ball until Tom smashes him into the netting. Then he comes on strong with a hammer.*

Some Chuck Jones cartoons were skimpy on plot. In Ah, Sweet Mouse-Story of Life, Jerry inexplicably comes up with a set of knives and pins Tom to the wall. Later in the same cartoon, Tom gets into a tight spot. The film's title is a play on that old Jeanette MacDonald/Nelson Eddy song, "Ah, Sweet Mystery of Life," but the story (or lack of) bears no resemblance.

A publicity still for Ah, Sweet Mouse-Story of Life.

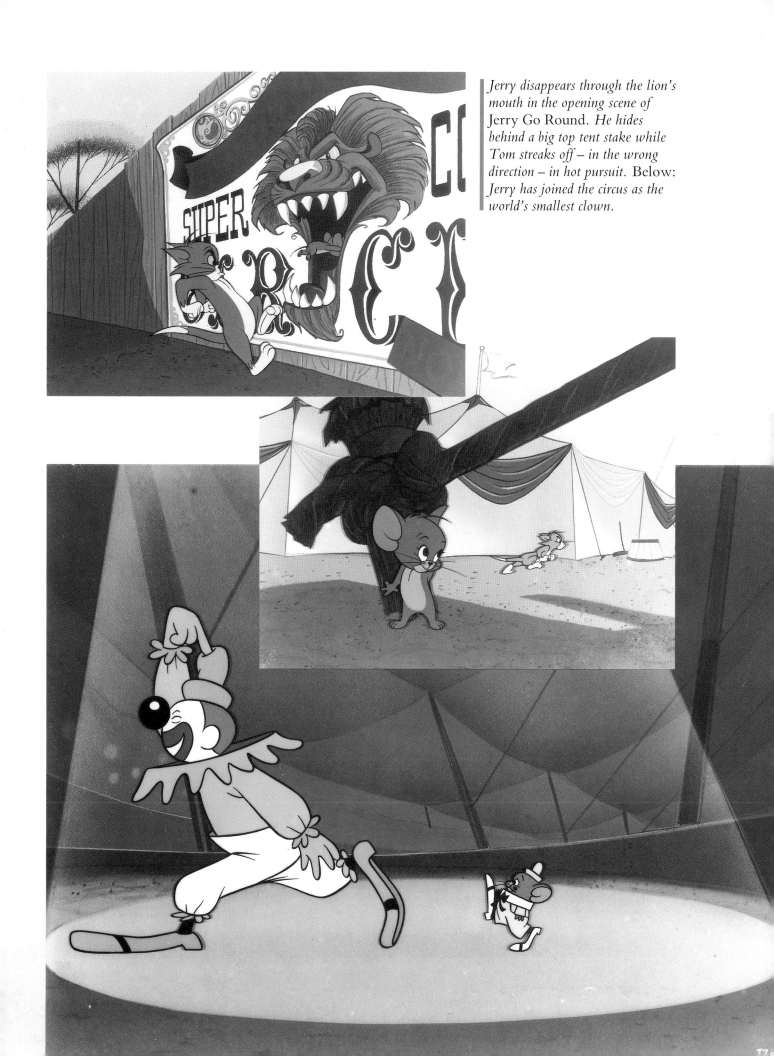

Jerry disappears through the lion's mouth in the opening scene of Jerry Go Round. *He hides behind a big top tent stake while Tom streaks off – in the wrong direction – in hot pursuit. Below: Jerry has joined the circus as the world's smallest clown.*

Jerry observes his sword with dismay after a brief fencing match with Tom in Duel Personality. *Below:* Another try. *In later scene from the same cartoon, the two face off with perfectly matched cannons — too well matched, for in the next scene the balls collide and the cannons roll backward, leaving both contestants unscathed.*

OF FELINE BONDAGE
Running Time 6.17 min. Release Date 1965

The title alludes to *Of Human Bondage*, a brooding MGM flick from 1964; the story is much lighter. A fairy princess gives Jerry a magic potion that renders him invisible. Tom's attempts to catch Jerry are thwarted when the unseen mouse scares the wits out of him with a pair of visible scissors. After both literally cut each other down to size, they laugh uproariously at their "sheared" appearance.

THE YEAR OF THE MOUSE
Running Time 7.23 min. Release Date 1965

The classic movie *Gaslight* retold, as Jerry and a nameless mouse buddy team up to make Tom think he's going crazy. He finds himself holding a smoking revolver, pointed at himself, wielding a knife

with fake blood on his chest, and suspended from the ceiling by a rope around his neck. At cartoon's end, however, Tom discovers the dastardly plot and traps both mice in a bottle from which there is no escape.

THE CAT'S ME-OUCH
Running Time 6.14 min. *Release Date* 1965

When Jerry buys a mouse-sized dog as a protector, Tom believes he's going to have a field day. But the tiny dog is too tough for the cat, who ends up in a hospital bed with both a bandage, and the miniature mutt, hanging onto his foot.

DUEL PERSONALITY
Running Time 6.09 min. *Release Date* 1966

Each having submitted his challenge card to the other, Tom and Jerry meet in a field to duel, using as weapons swords, pistols, bows and arrows, cannons and slingshots.

JERRY, JERRY QUITE CONTRARY
Running Time 7.17 min. *Release Date* 1966

Jerry's sleepwalking and Tom's in trouble. The little mouse, fearless in slumber, attacks the sleep-ing cat without waking – until Tom strikes back. Jerry tries drinking coffee to stay awake, but to no avail. Soon he's at it again, throwing Tom from the roof. Poor Tom can't take any more, packs his bag, and heads into the desert – but Jerry, still asleep, is following close behind.

JERRY GO-ROUND
Running Time 6.22 min. *Release Date* 1965

Circus highjinks as Jerry hides from Tom in the big top, disguised as a clown. When the little mouse pulls a nail out of an elephant's foot, he garners the grateful pachyderm's undying loyalty. Tom, still in pursuit, uses a variety of tricks but doesn't take into account the elephant's interference.

LOVE ME, LOVE MY MOUSE
Running Time 6.34 min. *Release Date* 1966

When the enamored Tom offers his girlfriend Jerry in a champagne cork, she protectively mothers the little mouse, repeatedly rescuing him from Tom's jaws. Then, kissing Jerry, she smacks her lips – and starts chasing him with a knife and fork.

In Puss 'n' Boats, *sailor Jerry is about to be awakened by the overpowering aroma of cheese.*

Only one shark goes after Jerry and then Tom in the film, but this publicity shot livened things up with two.

PUSS 'N' BOATS

Running Time 6.39 min. Release Date 1966

Shipboard shenanigans as watch cat Tom nabs Jerry trying to get to the cargo of cheese. A mad series of antics ensues, ending with Tom pursued out to sea by a shark and Jerry in a sailor suit, saluting the captain and dancing a jig.

FILET MEOW

Running Time 6.15 min. Release Date 1966

This fishy tale starts with Jerry rescuing a goldfish from Tom, goes on to relate how the cat ends up submerged in the basement, and ends with a shark in the bathtub.

MATINEE MOUSE

Running Time 6.07 min. Release Date 1966

This "wrap-around" cartoon uses sequences from vintage Hanna and Barbera era Tom & Jerrys in a story that has the cat and mouse at the movies, watching their earlier escapades. Egged on by the antics onscreen, they slam each other around in the theater seats, until the Tom and Jerry onscreen stop to watch the ones in the audience.

THE A-TOM-INABLE SNOWMAN

Running Time 6.39 min. Release Date 1966

In the Alps, Tom gets knocked out chasing Jerry and is revived, revitalized and intoxicated by a St Bernard with a keg of brandy. After several such episodes, Tom escapes with Jerry to a tropical island, where he is hit with a coconut. Not to worry – the St Bernard appears and renders his special brand of first aid.

CATTY CORNERED

Running Time 6.18 min. Release Date 1966

As Tom and a feline foe each attack Jerry, with a fly swatter, bows and arrows and explosives, through different entrances to a mousehole, both become convinced that a supermouse is inside, while Jerry, safely outside, munches on cheese. Finally both cats, having been the object of enough backfiring weapons, decide it's safer to move away. By now the mousehole is in ruins, so Jerry moves out, too.

CAT AND DUPLI-CAT

Running Time 6.45 min. Release Date 1967

Beneath a crescent moon, Tom and Jerry are singing "Santa Lucia" (and Tom is trying to swallow the mouse), when a shabby tabby appears. First mimicking Tom's actions and then vying with him for the possession of Jerry, the "dupli-cat" makes trouble for both Tom and Jerry, who manages to escape underwater, leaving his adversaries tied together.

O-SOLAR MEOW

Running Time 6.46 min. Release Date 1967

Tom and Jerry's Space Odyssey: living aboard a satellite, the chase continues, with the vehicle's gadgets used for weapons. When cat finally subdues mouse, he unwittingly sends him off in a spaceship to Limburger Crater, where Jerry feasts on the moon's greatest natural resource, cheese.

GUIDED MOUSE-ILLE

Running Time 6.45 min. Release Date 1967

The sequel to *O-Solar Meow*, this cartoon's official title includes the subtitle, "Or Science on a Wet Afternoon." In the year 2565, Tom and Jerry use mechanical replicas of themselves to do their battling. But with one futuristic blast too many, they blow themselves back to the Stone Age, where it all begins again.

Jerry makes himself at home behind the bar in typical Chuck Jones fashion. Notice the angelic cast to Jerry's face and Tom's fiendish eyebrows.

In Cat and Dupli-Cat, *Tom and his opponent see eye to eye – they both want Jerry (above). Top right: The two competitors fight over the prize. But Jerry has a surprise for them. Leaving them tied up (right), he slides into the water and away.*

In O-Solar Meow, *Tom and Jerry live in a space station that bears a curious resemblance to a roulette wheel. Left: Tom is enlarging Jerry's mouse hole with a laser gun when the jet-powered rodent races out to investigate. Later, Jerry sits down to a candlelit dinner in his cheese home, which is being powered through the space station by jet pack (below left). But Tom skewers the cheese with a harpoon and holds up its occupant (below). Two other cartoons used the same futuristic setting,* Guided Mouse-Ille *and* Advance and Be Mechanized.

ROCK 'N' RODENT
Running Time 6.22 min. Release Date 1967

Tom can't sleep for the noise from a cellar club combo in which Jerry stars on drums. His efforts to stop the noise only incur the wrath of a big bulldog, and when the racket finally ends and Jerry comes home to sleep, Tom's alarm goes off – it's time to get up.

CANNERY RODENT
Running Time 6.28 min. Release Date 1967

In a twist on John Steinbeck's "Cannery Row," Tom and Jerry find themselves tinned in a canning factory. Once out of their cans, they end up in the sea, pursued by a shark with cat – and mouse – food in mind.

THE MOUSE FROM H.U.N.G.E.R.
Running Time 6.47 min. Release Date 1967

Playing on the superspy craze of the day and MGM's own *The Man From U.N.C.L.E.*, superspy Jerry sets out in his roadster to capture a refrigerator full of cheese in a castle guarded by Tom (the cat from THRUSH). To stop Jerry, Tom sets up several explosive traps which all backfire, leaving Tom flat on his back while Jerry drives off with the refrigerator strapped to his roadster.

SURF-BORED CAT
Running Time 6.38 min. Release Date 1967

Tom is a way-out surfer cat, anxious to hang ten on some tough waves. But a shark, an octopus, and Jerry play havoc with his plans, and poor Tom, swallowing the surfboard, ends up riding the foam with Jerry on board.

SHUTTER BUGGED CAT
Running Time 6.48 min. *Release Date* 1967

Another "wrap-around" cartoon, this one has Tom reviewing old film footage (including *Designs on Jerry*) of his efforts to catch the mouse. The mouse, munching popcorn, watches along with him, and true to *Designs on Jerry*, changes one crucial figure when Tom goes to the drawing board and concocts a new mousetrap.

These two publicity shots appear to have been taken from The Year of the Mouse.

ADVANCE AND BE MECHANIZED
Running Time 6.33 min. *Release Date* 1967

Another space odyssey in which Tom and Jerry use cat and mouse robots to do the chasing. This time, the metal mechanos, tired of being bashed, switch roles with the furry feuders, and the real Tom and Jerry find themselves chasing each other.

PURR-CHANCE TO DREAM
Running Time 6.05 min. *Release Date* 1967

Tom is dreaming of a bulldog driving him into the ground when he is awakened by Jerry and a playful pup. Tom tries to rid himself of the pesky duo and, finally able to go back to sleep, picks up his dream where he left off, with the bulldog pounding him into the ground.

THE ALPHABETICAL CARTOON LIST

The years on this list reflect the copyright dates rather than release dates. The reader may note that they are not always the same.

One asterisk denotes a Chuck Jones production; two asterisks indicate direction by Gene Deitch with production by William L. Snyder. All others were directed by Hanna and Barbera and produced by Fred Quimby, except where noted.

Advance and Be Mechanized 1967
*Director: Ben Washam. Animation: Dick Thompson, Ben Washam, Don Towsley, Philip Roman

Ah, Sweet Mouse-Story of Life 1965
*Director: Chuck Jones. Animation: Dick Thompson, Ben Washam, Ken Harris, Don Towsley, Tom Ray

A-Tom-Inable Snowman 1967
*Director: Abe Levitow. Animation: Ken Harris, Don Towsley, Tom Ray, Dick Thompson, Ben Washam, Philip Roman

Baby Butch 1953
Animation: Irven Spence, Kenneth Muse, Ed Barge

Baby Puss 1943
Animation: Kenneth Muse, Ray Patterson, Irven Spence, Pete Burness

Bad Day at Cat Rock 1965
*Director: Chuck Jones. Animation: Ben Washam, Ken Harris, Don Towsley, Dick Thompson

Barbecue Brawl 1956
Producers: William Hanna, Joseph Barbera. Animation: Ed Barge, Irven Spence, Lewis Marshall, Kenneth Muse

Blue Cat Blues 1956
Producers: William Hanna, Joseph Barbera. Animation: Ed Barge, Irven Spence, Lewis Marshall, Kenneth Muse

The Bodyguard 1944
Animation: Kenneth Muse, Pete Burness, Ray Patterson, Irven Spence

The Bowling Alley-Cat 1942
No animation credits given.

The Brothers Carry-Mouse-Off 1966
*Director: Jim Pabian. Animation: Tom Ray, Dick Thompson, Ben Washam, Ken Harris, Don Towsley

Buddies Thicker Than Water 1962
No animation credits given.

Busy Buddies 1956
Producers: William Hanna, Joseph Barbera. Animation: Irven Spence, Lewis Marshall, Kenneth Muse, Ed Barge

Calypso Cat 1961
**Director of Animation: Vaclav Bedrich

Cannery Rodent 1967
*Director: Chuck Jones. Animation: Ben Washam, Ken Harris, Don Towsley, Tom Ray, Dick Thompson, O.E. Barkley, Bob Kirk

Carmen Get It! 1962
**No animation credits given.

Casanova Cat 1950
Animation: Irven Spence, Ray Patterson, Ed Barge, Kenneth Muse

The Cat Above, The Mouse Below 1964
*Director: Chuck Jones. Animation: Tom Ray, Dick Thompson, Ben Washam, Ken Harris, Don Towsley

Cat and Dupli-Cat 1967
*Director: Chuck Jones. Animation: Dick Thompson, Ben Washam, Ken Harris, Don Towsley, Tom Ray

The Cat and the Mermouse 1949
Animation: Kenneth Muse, Ed Barge, Ray Patterson, Irven Spence, Al Grandmain

The Cat Concerto 1946
Animation: Kenneth Muse, Ed Barge, Irven Spence

Cat Fishin' 1946
Animation: Kenneth Muse, Ed Barge, Michael Lah

Cat Napping 1951
Animation: Irven Spence, Ray Patterson, Ed Barge, Kenneth Muse

The Cat's Me-Ouch 1965
*Director: Chuck Jones. Animation: Don Towsley, Tom Ray, Dick Thompson, Ben Washam, Ken Harris

Catty-Cornered 1966
*Director: Abe Levitow. Animation: Tom Ray, Dick Thompson, Ben Washam, Ken Harris, Don Towsley

Cruise Cat 1951
Animation: Irven Spence, Ray Patterson, Ed Barge, Kenneth Muse

Cue Ball Cat 1950
Animation: Kenneth Muse, Irven Spence, Ed Barge, Ray Patterson

Designs on Jerry 1953
Animation: Irven Spence, Kenneth Muse, Ed Barge

Dicky Moe 1961
**Animation: Vaclav Bedrich

Dr. Jekyll and Mr. Mouse 1946
Animation: Ed Barge, Michael Lah, Kenneth Muse, Al Grandmain

The Dog House 1952
Animation: Kenneth Muse, Irven Spence, Ray Patterson, Ed Barge

Dog Trouble 1942
No animation credits given.

Down and Outing 1961
**No animation credits given.

Downbeat Bear 1956
Producers: William Hanna, Joseph Barbera. Animation: Kenneth Muse, Ed Barge, Irven Spence, Lewis Marshall

Downhearted Duckling 1953
Animation: Irven Spence, Ray Patterson, Kenneth Muse, Ed Barge

The Duck Doctor 1952
Animation: Irven Spence, Ray Patterson, Ed Barge, Kenneth Muse

Duel Personality 1967
*Director: Chuck Jones. Animation: Don Towsley, Tom Ray, Dick Thompson, Ben Washam, Ken Harris

The Egg and Jerry 1956
Producers: William Hanna, Joseph Barbera. Animation: Ed Barge, Ray Patterson, Irven Spence, Kenneth Muse

Feedin' the Kiddie 1956
Producers: William Hanna, Joseph Barbera. Animation: Irven Spence, Kenneth Muse, Ed Barge, Ray Patterson

Filet Meow 1967
*Director: Abe Levitow. Animation: Don Towsley, Tom Ray, Dick Thompson, Ben Washam, Ken Harris

Fine Feathered Friend 1942
Animation: Kenneth Muse, Pete Burness, George Gordon, Jack Zander, Bill Littlejohn

Fit To Be Tied 1952
Animation: Kenneth Muse, Irven Spence, Ray Patterson, Ed Barge

Flirty Birdy 1945
Animation: Irven Spence, Kenneth Muse, Ray Patterson

The Flying Cat 1951
Animation: Kenneth Muse, Irven Spence, Ed Barge, Ray Patterson

The Flying Sorceress 1955
Producers: William Hanna, Joseph Barbera. Animation: Ed Barge, Irven Spence, Lewis Marshall, Kenneth Muse

Fraidy Cat 1942
No animation credit given.

The Framed Cat 1950
Animation: Ed Barge, Kenneth Muse, Irven Spence, Ray Patterson

Guided Mouse-Ille 1966
*Director: Abe Levitow. Anima-tion: Don Towsley, Tom Ray, Dick Thompson, Ben Washam, Ken Harris, Philip Roman

Happy Go Ducky 1956
Producers: William Hanna, Joseph Barbera. Animation: Kenneth Muse, Bill Schipek, Ken Southworth, Herman Cohen, Lewis Marshall, James Escalante

Hatch Up Your Troubles 1948
Animation: Ed Barge, Ray Patterson, Irven Spence, Kenneth Muse

Haunted Mouse 1965
*Director: Chuck Jones. Animation: Ben Washam, Ken Harris, Don Towsley, Tom Ray, Dick Thompson

Heavenly Puss 1948
Animation: Ray Patterson, Irven Spence, Kenneth Muse, Ed Barge

Hic-cup Pup 1952
Animation: Ed Barge, Kenneth Muse, Ray Patterson, Irven Spence

High Steaks 1961
**Director of Animation: Vaclav Bedrich

His Mouse Friday 1951
Animation: Kenneth Muse, Irven Spence, Ray Patterson, Ed Barge

I'm Just Wild About Jerry 1965
*Director: Chuck Jones. Animation:
Dick Thompson, Ben Washam, Ken Harris, Don Towsley

The Invisible Mouse 1947
Animation: Ed Barge, Richard Bickenbach, Don Patterson, Irven Spence

Is There A Doctor in the Mouse? 1964
*Director: Chuck Jones. Animation: Ben Washam, Ken Harris, Don Towsley, Tom Ray, Dick Thompson

It's Greek to Me-Ow 1961
**No animation credits given.

Jerry and Jumbo 1951
Animation: Kenneth Muse, Irven Spence, Ed Barge

Jerry and the Goldfish 1951
Animation: Irven Spence, Ray Patterson, Ed Barge, Kenneth Muse

Jerry and the Lion 1950
Animation: Irven Spence, Ed Barge, Kenneth Muse, Ray Patterson

Jerry Go-Round 1965
*Director: Abe Levitow. Animation: Dick Thompson, Ben Washam, Ken Harris, Don Towsley, Tom Ray

Jerry, Jerry, Quite Contrary 1966
*Director: Chuck Jones. Animation: Ken Harris, Don Towsley, Tom Ray, Dick Thompson, Ben Washam, Al Pabian

Jerry's Cousin 1951
Animation: Ray Patterson, Ed Barge, Kenneth Muse, Irven Spence

Jerry's Diary 1949
Animation: Kenneth Muse, Ed Barge

Johann Mouse 1952
Animation: Kenneth Muse, Ray Patterson, Ed Barge, Irven Spence

Just Ducky 1951
Animation: Irven Spence, Ed Barge, Ray Patterson, Kenneth Muse, Al Grandmain

Kitty Foiled 1947
Animation: Irven Spence, Kenneth Muse, Irving Levine, Ed Barge

Landing Stripling 1961
**Director of Animation: Vaclav Bedrich

Life With Tom 1952
Animation: Kenneth Muse, Irven Spence, Ed Barge

The Little Orphan 1948
Animation: Irven Spence, Kenneth Muse, Ed Barge, Ray Patterson

Little Quacker 1950
Animation: Irven Spence, Ray Patterson, Ed Barge, Kenneth Muse

Little Runaway 1952
Animation: Ed Barge, Kenneth Muse, Irven Spence, Ray Patterson

Little School Mouse 1952
Animation: Irven Spence, Ed Barge

The Lonesome Mouse 1943
No animation credits given.

Love Me, Love My Mouse 1966
*Directors: Chuck Jones, Ben Washam. Animation: Ben Washam, Philip Roman, Don Towsley, Dick Thompson

Love That Pup 1949
Animation: Ed Barge, Ray Patterson, Irven Spence, Kenneth Muse

Matinee Mouse 1966
Director: Tom Ray. Animation: Ken Muse, Ed Barge, Irven Spence, Ray Patterson, Lewis Marshall. (Producer credit was given to MGM with additional director credit to Hanna and Barbera.)

Mice Follies 1953
Animation: Kenneth Muse, Ed Barge, Irven Spence, Ray Patterson

The Midnight Snack 1941
No animation credits given.

The Milky Waif 1946
Animation: Michael Lah, Kenneth Muse, Ed Barge

The Million Dollar Cat 1944
Animation: Irven Spence, Kenneth Muse, Pete Burness, Ray Patterson

The Missing Mouse 1952
Animation: Ray Patterson, Ed Barge, Kenneth Muse, Irven Spence

Mouse Cleaning 1948
Animation: Ray Patterson, Irven Spence, Kenneth Muse, Ed Barge

The Mouse Comes to Dinner 1945
Animation: Irven Spence, Kenneth Muse, Pete Burness, Ray Patterson

Mouse For Sale 1953
Animation: Kenneth Muse, Ed Barge, Irven Spence, Ray Patterson

The Mouse From H.U.N.G.E.R. 1967
★Director: Abe Levitow. Animation: Philip Roman, Ben Washam, Ken Harris, Don Towsley, Tom Ray, Dick Thompson

Mouse In Manhattan 1945
Animation: Kenneth Muse

A Mouse in the House 1947
Animation: Kenneth Muse, Ed Barge, Richard Bickenbach, Don Patterson

Mouse Into Space 1961
★★Director of Animation: Vaclav Bedrich

Mouse Trouble 1944
Animation: Ray Patterson, Irven Spence, Kenneth Muse, Pete Burness

Much Ado About Mousing 1964
★Director: Chuck Jones. Animation: Ben Washam, Ken Harris, Don Towsley, Tom Ray, Dick Thompson

Mucho Mouse 1956
Producers: William Hanna, Joseph Barbera. Animation: Lewis Marshall, Kenneth Muse, Bill Schipek, Jack Carr, Ken Southworth, Herman Cohen

Muscle Beach Tom 1956
Producers: William Hanna, Joseph Barbera. Animation: Lewis Marshall, Kenneth Muse, Ed Barge, Irven Spence

Neapolitan Mouse 1953
Animation: Ed Barge, Irven Spence, Ray Patterson, Kenneth Muse

The Night Before Christmas 1941
Animation: Kenneth Muse, Jack Zander, Pete Burness

Nit-Witty Kitty 1951
Animation: Ray Patterson, Ed Barge, Kenneth Muse, Irven Spence

Of Feline Bondage 1965
★Director: Chuck Jones. Animation: Ben Washam, Don Towsley, Ken Harris, Tom Ray, Dick Thompson

Old Rockin' Chair Tom 1947
Animation: Fred Barge, Ray Patterson, Iryen Spence, Kenneth Muse

O-Solar Meow 1966
★Director: Abe Levitow. Animation: Ken Harris, Don Towsley, Tom Ray, Dick Thompson, Ben Washam

Part Time Pal 1946
Animation: Michael Lah, Kenneth Muse, Ed Barge

Pecos Pest 1953
Animation: Ed Barge, Irven Spence, Ray Patterson, Kenneth Muse

Penthouse Mouse 1963
★Director: Chuck Jones. Animation: Ken Harris, Tom Ray, Dick Thompson, Ben Washam

Pet Peeve 1954
Animation: Ed Barge, Irven Spence, Kenneth Muse

Polka Dot Puss 1948
Animation: Kenneth Muse, Ed Barge, Ray Patterson, Irven Spence

Posse Cat 1952
Animation: Irven Spence, Ed Barge, Kenneth Muse, Ray Patterson

Professor Tom 1948
Animation: Ray Patterson, Irven Spence, Kenneth Muse, Ed Barge

Pup on a Picnic 1953
Animation: Ray Patterson, Kenneth Muse, Ed Barge, Irven Spence

Puppy Tale 1953
Animation: Ed Barge, Irven Spence, Kenneth Muse

Purr-Chance to Dream 1967
★Director: Ben Washam. Animation: Dick Thompson, Ken Harris, Don Towsley, Tom Ray, Philip Roman

Push-Button Kitty 1952
Animation: Irven Spence, Ed Barge, Kenneth Muse

Puss Gets the Boot 1940
Animation: Carl Urbano, Tony Pabian, Jack Zander, Pete Burness, Bob Allen

Puss 'n' Boats 1966
★Director: Abe Levitow. Animation: Ben Washam, Ken Harris, Don Towsley, Tom Ray, Dick Thompson

Puss 'n' Toots 1942
No animation credits given.

Puttin' On the Dog 1944
Animation: Pete Burness, Ray Patterson, Irven Spence, Kenneth Muse

Quiet Please 1945
Animation: Kenneth Muse, Ray Patterson, Irven Spence, Ed Barge

Robin Hoodwinked 1957
Producers: William Hanna, Joseph Barbera. Animation: Kenneth Muse, Carlo Vinci, Lewis Marshall, James Escalante

Rock 'n' Rodent 1967
★Director: Abe Levitow. Animation: Ben Washam, Dick Thompson, Tom Ray, Don Towsley, Ken Harris

Royal Cat Nap 1957
Producers: William Hanna, Joseph Barbera. Animation: Carlo Vinci, Lewis Marshall, Kenneth Muse

Safety Second 1950
Animation: Ray Patterson, Ed Barge, Kenneth Muse, Irven Spence, Al Grandmain

Salt Water Tabby 1947
Animation: Ed Barge, Michael Lah, Kenneth Muse

Saturday Evening Puss 1950
Animation: Ed Barge, Kenneth Muse, Irven Spence, Ray Patterson

Shutter Bugged Cat 1967
Director: Tom Ray. Animation: Irven Spence, Ed Barge, Ken Muse, George Gordon, Pete Burgess, Lewis Marshall, Ray Patterson. (Producer credit was given to MGM with additional director credit to Hanna and Barbera.)

Sleepy-Time Tom 1951
Animation: Ed Barge, Kenneth Muse, Irven Spence, Ray Patterson

Slicked-up Pup 1951
Animation: Ed Barge, Kenneth Muse, Irven Spence, Ray Patterson

Smarty Cat 1954
Animation: Irven Spence, Kenneth Muse, Ed Barge, Michael Lah

Smitten Kitten 1952
Animation: Kenneth Muse

Snowbody Loves Me 1964
★Director: Chuck Jones. Animation: Dick Thompson, Ben Washam, Ken Harris, Don Towsley, Tom Ray

Solid Serenade 1946
Animation: Ed Barge, Michael Lah, Kenneth Muse

Sorry Safari 1962
★★No animation credits given.

Southbound Duckling 1954
Animation: Kenneth Muse, Ed Barge, Irven Spence

Springtime for Thomas 1946
Animation: Ed Barge, Michael Lah, Kenneth Muse, Irven Spence (not credited)

Sufferin' Cats 1942
Animation: Kenneth Muse, George Gordon, Pete Burness, Jack Zander

Surf-Bored Cat 1967
*Director: Abe Levitow. Animation: Dick Thompson, Philip Roman, Ben Washam, Hal Ambro, Don Towsley, Carl Bell

Switchin' Kitten 1960
**Animation: Lu Guarnier, Gary Mooney

Tall in the Trap 1962
**No animation credits given.

Tee for Two 1945
Animation: Ray Patterson, Irven Spence, Peter Burness, Kenneth Muse

Tennis Chumps 1949
Animation: Ray Patterson, Irven Spence, Ed Barge, Kenneth Muse

Texas Tom 1950
Animation: Kenneth Muse, Ray Patterson, Irven Spence, Ed Barge

That's My Mommy 1955
Producers: William Hanna, Joseph Barbera. Animation: Kenneth Muse, Ed Barge, Irven Spence, Lewis Marshall

That's My Pup 1952
Animation: Kenneth Muse, Ray Patterson, Ed Barge, Irven Spence

Timid Tabby 1956
Producers: William Hanna, Joseph Barbera. Animation: Lewis Marshall, Kenneth Muse, Irven Spence, Ken Southworth, Bill Schipek

Tom and Cherie 1955
Animation: Irven Spence, Kenneth Muse, Lewis Marshall, Ed Barge

The Tom and Jerry Cartoon Kit 1961
**Director of Animation: Vaclav Bedrich

Tom and Jerry in the Hollywood Bowl 1950
Animation: Kenneth Muse, Irven Spence, Ray Patterson, Ed Barge

Tom-Ic Energy 1964
*Director: Chuck Jones. Animation: Ken Harris, Don Towsley, Tom Ray, Dick Thompson, Ben Washam

Tom's Photo Finish 1956
Producers: William Hanna, Joseph Barbera. Animation: Kenneth Muse, Bill Schipek, Lewis Marshall, Jack Carr, Herman Cohen, Ken Southworth

Tops with Pops 1956
Producers: William Hanna, Joseph

Barbera. Animation: Ed Barge, Ray Patterson, Irven Spence, Kenneth Muse

Tot Watchers 1957
Producers: William Hanna, Joseph Barbera. Animation: Lewis Marshall, James Escalante, Kenneth Muse

Touche, Pussy Cat 1954
Animation: Kenneth Muse, Ed Barge, Irven Spence

Trap Happy 1946
Animation: Kenneth Muse, Ed Barge, Michael Lah

Triplet Trouble 1952
Animation: Ray Patterson, Ed Barge, Kenneth Muse, Irven Spence

The Truce Hurts 1947
Animation: Kenneth Muse, Ed Barge, Ray Patterson, Irven Spence

Two Little Indians 1952
Animation: Ray Patterson, Kenneth Muse, Irven Spence, Ed Barge

The Two Mouseketeers 1952
Animation: Ed Barge, Kenneth Muse, Irven Spence

The Unshrinkable Jerry Mouse 1964
*Director: Chuck Jones. Animation: Dick Thompson, Ben Washam, Ken Harris, Don Towsley, Tom Ray

The Vanishing Duck 1957
Producers: William Hanna, Joseph Barbera. Animation: Lewis Marshall, Kenneth Muse, Carlo Vinci, James Escalante

The Yankee Doodle Mouse 1943
Animation: Irven Spence, Pete Burness, Kenneth Muse, George Gordon

The Year of the Mouse 1965
*Director: Chuck Jones. Animation: Dick Thompson, Ben Washam, Ken Harris, Don Towsley .

The Zoot Cat 1944
Animation: Ray Patterson, Kenneth Muse, Irven Spence, Pete Burness

Index

Page numbers in *italics* refer to captions for illustrations